GUWAHATI – THE GATEWAY TO THE EAST

About the Editors

Dr. K. Alam is a senior Professor of Economics, Gauhati University. He was a member of Assam Public Service Commission for a term. He edited a number of books, including *Planning in North East India*. He contributed a large number of research papers to many research journals in the Country. He was a former President of NEICSSR for two terms.

Dr. N.C. Das a senior Professor of Commerce, and a former Dean of Gauhati University is an eminent research guide. He is associated with number of Universities and was a Co-ordinator for World Bank Project. He contributed about 50 research papers in national and international journals. He edited a number of books. Currently he is the President of North East India Council for Social Science Research, a pioneering research organisation in India.

Dr. A.K. Borah is a faculty member in the Department of Sociology, Dibrugarh University. He contributed a large number of research papers to many journals and publicaitons. Dr. Borah is specialised in Urban studies and in social welfare administration and actively participated in many national seminar.

GUWAHATI

The Gateway to the East

Editors

K. ALAM
N.C. DAS
A.K. BORAH

CONCEPT PUBLISHING COMPANY, NEW DELHI - 110059

ISBN 81-7022-876-X

First Published 2001

Published and Printed by

Ashok Kumar Mittal
Concept Publishing Company
A/15-16, Commercial Block, Mohan Garden,
NEW DELHI -110059 (India)

Phones : 5648039, 5649024
Fax : 091-11-5648053
Email : *publishing@conceptpub.com*

PREFACE

With Political reorganisation of North-East India in 1972, the capital of Assam was shifted to Guwahati from Shillong which became the capital of Meghalaya, the new Hill state. This decision was political one and the town of Guwahati was not ready for it. It resulted confusion and chaos in Guwahati Urban Growth and Management. The academicians, social scientists, engineers, town planners and researchers in a workshop at Guwahati in November 1999 examined and analysed the issues and problems of urban growth and management in a scientific study and contributed to the possible solution to the complex sociological and urban planning of problems of growing city in North East India. This study is unique in historical perspection.

Professor K. Alam, Professor N.C. Das and Dr. A.K. Borah are well known economists and sociologists respectively. We are grateful to them for the arduous task undertaken by them in editing this volume. We are thankful to Mr. Ashok Kumar Mittal of Concept Publishing Company, New Delhi for undertaking this publication responsibility.

20 March 2000.

B. Datta Ray
Secretary
North East India Council
for Social Science Research,
Shillong- 793003

INTRODUCTION

Guwahati had never been a political Head Quarters of Assam during the Ahom period nor during the British occupation since 1826. All Commissioners of Assam, a Revenue Division of Bengal Government were extremely careful in avoiding Guwahati, a place considered extremely insanitory and malarious. When Assam was separated from Bengal, as a separate entity, under the Supreme Government of India as a Chief Commissioner's Province in 1874, Guwahati remained Headquarters of this new Province for the initial 40 days as it was considered that Shillong was the only place fit to be political and administrative Head Quarters of the Province of Assam for health of the colonial people and for strategic and administrative reasons.

With the reorganisation of North East India in 1972 when Meghalaya was created as a distinct State of the Union of India, a momentous decision was taken by the State Government of Assam in 1972, operating from Shillong to shift the capital of Assam from Shillong to Guwahati. The choice of Dispur, a road side village with paddy fields all around near the town of Guwahati, the district Headquarters of Kamrup proved to be an ecological disaster. This decision was political and administrative, ecological consideration was not taken into account very seriously for building make shift temporary structures of typical Assam type. At a war footing structures were built and by phases office started moving to the new capital of Assam with short-term and long-term –ecological, political, economic and social consequences.

Guwahati has always been a gateway to North East India and particularly since Independence, it became political and economic nerve centre. With the construction and opening of Saraighat Bridge across the mighty Brahmaputra economic development process was accelerated and outside capital flowed in Guwahati and organised tea auction market grew. The new second oil refinary project started in creating a new auxiliary industrial growth centres around Guwahati. The establishment of Gauhati University in 1948 and its shifting to permanent campus at Jalukhbari in Nineteen fifties and Maligaon becoming Head Quarters of North East Frontier Railways with its network and its conversion into broad gauge and with radical growth of population, the phase of Guwahati urbanisation was rapid. The growth of professional institutions, Medical, Dental, Aurvedic and Engineering Colleges along with a rapid growth of under-graduate, higher secondary and secondary educational institutions the face of Guwahati became cosmopolitan. With the coming of Radio Station and Television Centre and with the growth of a large number of newspapers, libraries and cultural institutions, the character of Guwahati changed almost beyond recognition.

The total area of Greater Guwahati is about 243.2 sq. km. including North Guwahati of 23 sq. km. area located on the northern bank of the river Brahmaputra. The total population of Greater Guwahati is over half a million. Tremendous increase of population during last couple of decades pose serious problems to the Guwahati city. Influx of the immigrant both from inside and outside the state into the city is the prime factor of population explosion. Shifting of capital from Shillong to Dispur, establishment of new industries and growth of commercial activities increased the problems. Filling up of lowlying areas for residential establishments, growth of several new colonies led to the abrupt and abnormal expansion of the city. Unplanned growth of city functions resulted into a chaotic Urban situation.

The topography of Greater Guwahati controlling the natural drainage, becomes ineffective during the flood seasons every year. Backflow of mighty Brahmaputra through its outlets like Bharalu, causes flood frequently in every summer. Waterlogging of streets and the spillout of drainwater, together with rain and sewerage, flood the vast areas of the city of Guwahati. The city transport and power situation is dismal.

With increasing industrial and commercial activities in and around Greater Guwahati, air, water and soil pollution have grown in alarming proportion which have raised serious concerns. The ecology in totality has been destroyed by clearing original vegetation by wanton felling of trees. Hill cutting for earth and blasting rocks endangered the flora and fauna of Greater Guwahati.

In this scenario of chaos and confusion in Guwahati urban growth and activities, academicians, social scientists, engineers, town planners and research scholars in a seminar in 1999 examined and analysed the issues and problems in a scientific manner and thereby contributed to its planned growth for prosperity, health and welfare of Guwahati

K. Alam
N.C. Das
A.K. Borah

CONTENTS

LIST OF CONTRIBUTORS

Pabitra Giri
Centre for Urban Economic Studies, Calcutta University, Calcutta - 700027.

N.N. Bhattacharyya
Department of Geography, Gauhati University, Guwahati - 781014

K.M. Deka
Department of Political Science, Dibrugarh University, Dibrugarh-786004.

H. Nath
Environment Engineering Consultant, Guwahati.

D. Bhattacharjee
Public Health Engineering Department, Government of Assam, Guwahati.

S. Bezbaruah
Guwahati Municipal Corporation, Guwahati.

Kamlesh Kalita
Department of Geography, Gauhati University, Guwahati-781014.

Aswini Kr. Borah
Department of Sociology, Dibrugarh University, Dibrugarh-786004.

Kabindra Hazarika
Public Works Department, Government of Assam, Guwahati.

S. Sharma
Department of Geography, North Eastern Hill University,
Shillong-793014.

M. Kar
Department of Geography, Nowgong College,
Haibargaon- 782002, Assam.

S. Br. Medhi
National Human Rights Commission, Kharghuli,
Guwahati - 781004.

K. Bez
Institute of Econometrics and Applied Statistics,
Hengerabari, Guwahati- 781036.

C. Sharma
Gopal Boro H.S. School, Guwahati.

A.K. Afsar Hazarika
North Eastern Development Financial Corporation,
Guwahati-781005.

Amiyo Kr. Sharma
N.E.D.F.I., Guwahati-781005.

S.K. Sarmah
Environmental Science Scholar, Arya Nagar,
Guwahati- 781016.

P. Dattabarua
Department of Chemistry, Guwahati College, Guwahati.

Pradip Sharma
Department of Geography, Cotton College, Guwahati.

Mahfuza Rahaman
Department of Geography, Cotton College, Guwahati.

Monalisa Choudhury
Department of Commerce, Dispur College,
Guwahati- 781006.

Nayan Barua
Department of Commerce, Gauhati University,
Guwahati- 781014.

B. Datta Ray
N.E.I.C.S.S.R., Shillong.

Gayatree Goswamee
Department of Education, Gauhati University,
Guwahati - 781014.

Mini Bhattacharyya Thakur
Department of Anthropology, Gauhati University,
Guwahati- 781014.

Polly Vauquline
Bajali College, Pathsala, Barpeta, Assam.

Taranee Deka
Department of English, B.B. Kishan College, Jalah,
Barpeta, Assam.

Circles. Besides, Imphal East District have 3 (three) Community Development Blocks, viz., (i) Imphal East – I, (ii) Imphal East – II and (iii) Jiribam and Imphal West District have 2 (two) of the same viz., (1) Imphal West – I and (2) Imphal West – II for the implementation of development schemes.

Need of the Present Study

The development of the Indian economy has lead to a rise in unemployment mostly because of the mismatch between creations of employment and the addition to labour force. Therefore, expansion of avenues of self-employment within rural areas is one of the major ways of reviving the rural economy. The rural non-farm sector has the potential to link the country side with the towns as well as the promise of becoming the most dynamic part of the economy.

In view of the above, the paper seeks to analyse the socio economic origins of rural entrepreneurs of Imphal East and Imphal West districts of Manipur.

Objectives of the Study

The specific objectives of the study are as follows:

1. To enquire into socio-economic origins of the rural entrepreneurship in SMEs in the Imphal East and Imphal West Districts of Manipur.
2. To analyse the problems and prospects of rural entrepreneurship in the said two districts.
3. To recommend some possible suggestions for the growth and development of rural entrepreneurship in Manipur.

Research Design

The sampled entrepreneurs are taken from registered small scale industries of rural areas of Imphal East and Imphal West districts

1

DEMOGRAPHIC AND ECONOMIC CHANGES IN GUWAHATI SINCE 1972

Pabitra Giri

Guwahati since 1972 has been the capital of the reorganised State of Assam. Before 1972 it was never a state headquarter in modern times except for a brief period, though in ancient times the area was location of various pre-historic urban settlements. In this paper, we first consider the factors that could have influenced the growth of Guwahati since 1972. The first issue is how urban development of Guwahati had been influenced as it became the state Capital. As a Headquarter of the State Administration, the city became the central place of the state with respect to various government services. As it always happened, the state Capital is better linked in terms of transport and communication, not only with the districts of the state but also with urban centres outside the state. Therefore, Guwahati have gradually acquired an extended hinterland which crossed the territorial boundary of the reorganised Assam State. Besides being a state capital it has a more intensive linkage with its hinterland. Secondly, overtime Guwahati became the gateway to the north-east India. It became a centre of various public investments and concomitant private investments. These factors contributed to enormous demographic growth of Guwahati during 1971–91 as can be seen from Table 1.1. Moreover, Guwahati registered relatively faster growth compared to the other cities and towns of Assam. The growing dominance of the city is reflected in its rising share (from 9.60% in 1971 to 23.22% in 1991) in the urban population of Assam. Further, the huge demographic growth over a relatively short period is contributed by permanent migration of families rather than lone male migration is apparent from the rise in the gender ratio (measured as females per thousand males) from 638 in 1971 to 783 in 1991.

Table 1.1 : Growth profile of Guwahati in relation to urban growth in Assam

Year	Population (000)	Gender Ratio	Decadal growth	Share (%) in urban population of Assam
1901	11.6	500	–	15.13
1911	12.5	534	7.03	13.43
1921	16.5	528	32.04	12.97
1931	21.8	503	32.26	13.44
1941	29.6	567	35.79	14.22
1951	43.6	558	47.36	12.65
1961	100.7	497	130.90*	12.89
1971	123.7	638	22.90	9.60
1981	200.3	755	61.87	11.24
1991	557.6	783	188.25	23.22
2001	1141.0**			

*Extension of municipal boundary.

**Estimated by linear projection.

One important question is whether the fast demographic growth of Guwahati had been complemented by an adequate economic prosperity. One way of dealing with this issue is to ask whether there were growing job opportunities in Guwahati. The work participation rate (number of workers to total population) in Guwahati increased only marginally from 32.3 percent in 1971 to 33.2 percent in 1991. Further, if we exclude the marginal workers (0.28 percent of population) the increase in work participation rate was just by

0.6 percent. Anyway the proportion of working population had increased in the city during 1971–91, but it would not be proper to infer the nature of economic change from the increased proportion of workers. It is important to know in which sectors the employment had increased. We, therefore, consider the change in workforce structure in Guwahati during 1971-1991 (Table 1.2). During these two decades, though the number of manufacturing workers has increased but the share of manufacturing in the total workers decreased slightly. It can be further noted that the shares of "trade and commerce" and "other services" – including various services from public administration to domestic service-sectors had increased. Guwahati has developed more as a trading and administrative centre while industry took a back seat in the urban development of the city. The workforce has increased more than proportionately in the sectors in which informal low productivity activities were present in large proportion. Therefore, one can suggest that the rapid population growth of Guwahati had not been accompanied by a parallel expansion in its economy – particularly the high productivity manufacturing activities have not expanded.

Table 1.2 : Workforce Structure of Guwahati, 1971 and 1991

	1971		1991	
	(number)	(% share)	(number)	(% share)
Total Workers	65969	100.00	194079	100.00
Cultivators	546	0.83	2601	1.34
Agricultural labour	266	0.40	2044	1.05
Livestock, plantation etc.	628	0.95	4819	2.48
Mining & quarrying	25	0.04	876	0.45
Household manufacturing	950	1.44	1260	0.65
Non-household manufacturing	8565	12.98	21642	11.15
Construction	2529	3.83	10518	5.42
Trade & commerce	14455	21.91	50546	26.04
Transport & communication	15259	23.13	27335	14.08
Other services	22746	34.48	72438	37.32

Source : Census of India 1971 and 1991.

The change in the pattern of migration in Guwahati between 1971 and 1991 also indicates the nature of economic changes during the period. Table 1.3 shows the pattern of migration by place of last residence, in Guwahati City in 1971 and in 1991. The proportion of migrants in the resident population has declined over the years from 58.79 percent in 1971 to 47.38 percent in 1991. It can be seen that the proportion of migrants from within Assam had increased while the share of migrants from the other states of India and outside India had decreased between 1971 and 1991. In 1991 more than 62 percent of intra-state migrants to Guwahati had come from the rural areas (Table 1.4). Further, it may be noted that of the rural-urban migrants only about 32 percent migrated for employment and business; while about eight percent for education. The increase in the proportion of relatively short distance rural-urban migration is usually associated with the proliferation of informal sector low productivity activities. It can be observed further that those who had come for business purpose, more than 50 percent were from outside Assam.

Table 1.3 : Change in the pattern of migration in Guwahati City

	1971	1991
Proportion of migrants		
Persons	58.79	47.38
Males	63.46	48.19
Females	51.86	46.34
Total migrants	100.00	100.00
Resident in India	83.12	95.40
Intra-State	49.42	66.30
Within district	25.92	14.60
Between districts	23.50	51.70
Inter-State	33.71	29.10
From Bihar	11.97	n.a
Uttar Pradesh	3.48	n.a
Rajasthan	2.33	n.a
West Bengal	6.83	n.a
Outside India	16.88	4.60

Source : Census of India, 1971 and 1991.

Note : Based on migration data by place of last residence.

Table 1.4 : Percentage distribution of migrants (last residence) by origin of migration in Guwahati, 1991

	Total	Employment	Business
Total	100.0	100.0	100.0
A. Last Residence in India			
Total	95.4	97.2	95.4
Rural	54.8	60.7	59.3
Urban	40.0	36.3	35.1
1. Migrants from within Assam			
Total	66.3	74.5	47.9
Rural	41.2	49.0	30.8
Urban	24.8	25.4	17.0
1a. Migrants from within district			
Total	14.6	15.8	9.5
Rural	12.2	13.6	7.7
Urban	2.4	2.2	1.8
1b. Migrants from other districts of state			
Total	51.7	58.6	38.4
Rural	29.1	35.3	23.1
Urban	22.4	23.1	15.2
2. Migrants from other states of India			
Total	29.1	22.8	47.5
Rural	13.6	11.7	28.5
Urban	15.2	10.9	18.2
B. Last Residence outside India	4.6	2.8	4.6

Source : Census of India' 1991 : Migration Tables for Assam

Table 1.6 shows the labour force participation rate and unemployment rate of Guwahati for various age groups and for males and females. The unemployment rates are relatively high in the lower age groups for both males and females. It is surprising to note that among the children, in the age group of 5–14, who were outside the formal labour force, the unemployment rate is about 21 percent, while for the labour force (age group 15–59) it was near about nine percent. Thus, for a good number of children either they themselves were searching for jobs or their parents were willing to put them on work.

This was also indicative of very low income for a good number of households in the city. In general, female unemployment rate (proportion of those willing to work but not getting work to those who are available for work, i.e., either working or searching for work) was higher for males than for females in Guwahati in 1991. One interesting observation is that while unemployment rate declined in general as we moved from younger age groups to middle and older age groups for both male and female, the unemployment rate for female remained much higher than that for males in the middle age group. It implies that many of the urban women either search for jobs or feels that they can enter in the job market at a relatively higher age.

Table 1.5 : Distribution of Migrants (by place of last residence) in Guwahati by reasons for migration, 1991

	Total	Employment	Business	Education	Family	Marriage	Natural calamities	Others
Total	100.0	22.0	8.8	6.0	22.5	17.3	0.4	22.9
A. Last residence in India								
Total	100.0	22.4	8.8	6.3	22.3	17.5	0.4	22.3
Rural	100.0	24.3	9.6	6.6	20.6	17.1	0.4	21.4
Urban	100.0	19.9	7.8	5.9	24.8	18.0	0.4	23.2
1. Migrants from within Assam								
Total	100.0	24.7	6.4	7.5	20.8	18.6	0.3	21.7
Rural	100.0	26.1	6.6	7.9	19.5	18.1	0.4	21.5
Urban	100.0	22.5	6.0	7.0	23.1	19.6	0.3	21.6
1a. Migrants from within district								
Total	100.0	23.8	5.8	7.1	18.4	21.2	0.4	23.3
Rural	100.0	24.6	5.6	7.4	18.4	20.3	0.4	23.2
Urban	100.0	20.2	6.6	5.4	17.9	25.6	0.6	23.6
1b. Migrants from other districts in Assam								
Total	100.0	24.9	6.6	7.6	21.5	17.9	0.3	21.2
Rural	100.0	26.7	7.0	8.0	19.9	17.2	0.3	20.8
Urban	100.0	22.7	6.0	7.1	23.6	18.9	0.2	21.4
2. Migrants from other states in India								
Total	100.0	17.2	14.4	3.5	25.8	14.8	0.5	23.8
Rural	100.0	19.0	18.6	2.8	24.1	14.0	0.4	21.1
Urban	100.0	15.8	10.6	4.1	27.6	15.5	0.5	25.9
B. Last residence outside India								
Total	100.0	13.2	8.8	1.2	27.0	14.1	0.0	35.7

Table 1.6 : Labour force participation rate and unemployment rate in Guwahati by sex and age, 1991

Age group	Labour force participation rate			Unemployment rate		
	Total	Male	Female	Total	Male	Female
Total	36.82	56.33	11.91	9.05	6.62	23.71
5-14	6.07	5.10	7.07	21.39	27.74	16.69
15-19	18.90	27.16	8.75	22.87	18.30	40.31
20-24	39.82	58.72	15.69	24.58	19.89	47.02
25-29	66.61	88.29	19.84	12.52	9.50	28.12
30-34	64.27	95.77	22.17	5.62	3.85	15.83
35-39	64.31	97.41	16.41	2.42	1.37	11.42
40-49	69.39	96.43	18.25	1.57	0.93	8.01
50-59	62.90	91.03	10.08	1.21	0.41	14.78
60-69	30.88	50.09	3.31	4.84	4.14	20.00
70-79	22.20	38.71	0.43	4.13	4.17	0.00
80+	19.37	32.67	4.48	16.36	14.29	33.33
Age n.s.	15.60	23.65	3.92	25.64	22.86	50.00
15-59	52.36	78.17	16.27	8.67	6.27	24.81
60+	27.41	45.47	2.77	5.71	4.97	22.22

Source : Census of India 1991.
Note : Age n.s. = age not stated.

Table 1.7 provides ward-wise data on Guwahati City in 1991. There were 34 wards in the city. It can be observed that some of the wards (Ward Nos. 19, 2, 1, 7, 3, 8, 12, 13, 17, 18, 20, 21) were worst hit by overcrowding as number of persons per residential households exceed the city average of 4.67 persons per residential house. In some of the wards, which showed overcrowding, the gender-ratio (females per thousand males) was remarkably low indicating the concentration of lone male migrants. For example, Ward No. 19 had lowest gender ratio (599) followed by 21 (665). On the other hand in some wards the gender ratio were more than 900, indicating that these areas are primarily residential quarters, where lone male migrants were small in number.

Table 1.7 : World-wise data on Guwahati City

Ward No.	Pop/Res. House	Gender Ratio	Lit rate Male	Lit rate Female	WPR Male	WPR Female	WPR Total	% of Nhh Mfg	% of HH Mfg
1.	5.87	912	73.79	62.07	36.86	2.94	20.68	4.28	0.93
2.	6.71	715	80.92	68.00	42.30	10.35	28.98	4.46	0.62
3.	5.16	821	67.43	60.20	50.04	4.50	29.50	5.21	0.97
4.	4.86	833	79.76	68.94	49.46	5.35	29.41	8.73	0.34
5.	4.88	906	77.23	66.56	48.48	11.87	31.07	2.12	0.63
6.	4.98	863	78.81	70.36	48.62	6.78	29.24	7.69	0.87
7.	5.66	839	77.16	68.30	54.01	5.99	32.10	12.71	0.31
8.	5.15	918	84.04	75.05	45.84	12.61	29.93	2.02	0.90
9.	4.87	837	75.08	62.17	47.95	8.17	29.83	12.36	0.93
10.	5.00	835	63.96	49.61	50.01	4.39	29.25	24.92	2.73
11.	4.95	836	71.56	59.88	51.58	6.52	31.06	18.75	2.52
12.	5.35	767	71.61	68.68	56.56	9.73	36.22	10.24	0.88
13.	5.79	759	75.16	70.02	56.00	4.77	33.90	14.10	1.39
14.	4.65	797	74.64	65.83	51.58	4.28	30.60	25.32	0.41
15.	4.76	798	78.14	67.02	49.61	7.36	30.87	10.58	0.18
16.	4.17	778	73.69	66.84	54.28	10.06	34.93	10.34	0.34
17.	5.11	831	81.81	74.61	54.98	10.34	34.72	9.95	0.31
18.	5.55	724	79.62	72.97	59.37	8.40	37.96	12.62	0.17
19.	6.68	599	75.49	72.10	59.50	2.57	38.18	7.64	0.16

(Contd.)

Table 1.7 : (*Contd.*)

Ward No.	Pop/Res. House	Gender Ratio	Lit rate Male	Lit rate Female	WFR Male	WPR Female	WPR Total	% of Nhh Mfg	% of HH Mfg
20.	5.58	687	72.56	71.59	59.94	10.65	39.88	5.35	0.00
21.	5.46	665	78.34	69.90	57.07	11.51	38.87	6.21	0.45
22.	4.73	757	72.07	63.28	56.84	11.14	37.15	9.44	0.92
23.	4.36	791	73.89	64.78	54.90	9.56	34.88	7.89	0.29
24.	4.38	885	77.13	67.29	51.56	16.11	34.92	6.23	0.35
25.	4.70	823	77.64	68.96	54.42	12.84	35.65	8.50	0.83
26.	4.49	770	78.01	67.17	54.13	11.52	35.60	10.40	0.62
27.	4.12	773	83.37	73.00	49.41	10.38	32.40	10.76	0.69
28.	4.71	814	85.91	75.23	54.88	16.14	37.50	8.02	0.20
29.	4.21	780	78.97	69.05	51.37	11.04	33.70	11.99	0.24
30.	4.17	742	79.83	68.75	52.37	7.41	33.23	12.24	0.37
31.	4.[illegible]2	781	75.61	59.83	48.74	6.21	30.09	28.04	0.27
32.	4.22	789	69.81	55.10	50.73	8.02	31.90	12.34	0.43
33.	4.48	660	74.88	58.89	59.55	8.78	39.36	5.90	0.56
34.	4.23	760	73.09	59.36	56.02	11.64	36.85	5.44	0.30
City Total	4.67	783	75.50	64.42	52.40	8.71	33.21	11.15	0.60

Literacy rate was quite high in Guwahati both for male and female compared to many other urban centres in the country. However, in some of the wards, female literacy rate was low as also the female work participation rate. The work participation rate varied across the wards. It was highest in ward 20 (39.88) and lowest in ward 1 (20.68). This was most likely due to the residential segregation of various economic and social groups who did not have either similar access to labour markets or same rate of labour force participation. It is interesting to note that wards with relatively high incidence of non-household manufacturing had lower work participation rate. However, exact reasons cannot be identified without further research.

In fine, given the geographical location of Guwahati *vis-à-vis* the rest of India and the nature of transport network that emerged after partition, the town was most likely to expand. However, after being selected as the site of the capital of the state, the town quickly transformed itself into a large city. Urban growth, in terms of population, was phenomenal as it became the central place of the Assam for transport, trade and administration like Calcutta in the case of West Bengal. Guwahati might not be right choice for the location of the state capital from an environmental perspective. However, in a capital poor country, location decisions are often influenced by the availability of the existing transport infrastructure rather than the environmental considerations. The fast growth of Guwahati in relatively a short period, with- out adequate economic growth, might have aggravated the environmental and ecological problems, for which viable solutions might not exist in near future.

2

GROWTH AND CHANGING FACE OF GUWAHATI SINCE 1972

N.N. Bhattacharyya

The modern Guwahati has been identified as the ancient Pragjyotishpura. But there are no sufficient evidence and pedantic argument to support it. However, ancient Guwahati was the flourishing capital of several dynasties during the epic and classical period. It had never been the capital city of the Ahom kingdom nor the Koch kingdom. The strategic importance of Guwahati was well known to the Moghul invaders. In 1667, the Moghul forces were defeated in a battle by the Ahom forces commanded by the illustrious Lachit Barphukan. Thus, in a sense Guwahati became the bone of contention among the Ahoms, Kochas and the Moghuls during the medieval period. The Ahom king made Guwahati the administrative headquarters of Lower Assam with a Viceroy or a Barphukan. Modern Guwahati dates back to the British occupation of Assam in 1826 and it is from this date the city came to have due importance. Except few temples, an earthen fort and tanks there are hardly any medieval remnants and ruins in Guwahati. The sectors Fancy Bazar, Panbazar and Ujan bazar form a contiguous and relatively compact area. This may be called kernel of the city which is dominated by traditional morphological features of a typical oriental town renovated during British occupation of this area. The later urban structures are arranged as a very irregular and discontinuous zone round the kernel in its south, west and east, but the presence of the Brahmaputra does not allow accretion to the north. The non-contiguous and isolated physical barriers such as the small hills and marshes and the narrow channel of the Bharalu stream lie in between the urban appendages. The general picture of growth shows some dissimilarities between the various parts of the city's built-up area.

It is to be noted that throughout the 19th century and also during the first four decades of the 20th century the growth of Guwahati was very slow. But, thereafter, both spatial and population growth of the city was rather rapid. During the World War-II the Britishers used this city as their strongholds by establishing the civil lines and cantonments. The significant development during the British period was the establishment of the cantonment at Paltan bazar, opening new lines of transport and communication and improvement of old ones within the town which imparted and added to the city. This then was followed by the independence of the country and since then Guwahati has undergone a remarkable change and the present expansion of the city is the result of agglomeration of urban structures developed around multiple nuclei. The significant development which ever took place in the evolutional history of Guwahati were establishment of the High Court, the Railway Headquarters, the University Campus, the Engineering College, the Medical College, the construction of Saraighat bridge, oil refinery, military cantonment at Satgaon, the Industrial Estate, many Central and State Government offices and institutions etc. and all these were during the early sixties. Just after independence, a large number of refugees from the erstwhile East Pakistan came to settle here with their families. These factors coupled with an ever increasing stream of men from various parts of India came to Guwahati in search of employment which rendered a spectacular growth of urban population in Guwahati. In accordance with this economic and social backgroud the population of Guwahati increased rapidly during the modern period. During the decade of 1951–1961, Guwahati recorded an increase of population of 130.9 percent i.e. from 43,615 (1931) to 1,00,707 (1961). It rose to 1,23,783 in 1971 and in the area of Guwahati Municipal Corporation the population was 2,00,377 (1971) which was 16 percent of the total urban population of Assam. The tempo of growth and the development of the city was further enhanced during the next few years with the setting up of temporary capital complex at Dispur near Guwahati. In 1972, about 20,000 people including their families came to Guwahati from Shillong along with shifting of capital of Assam from Shillong to Guwahati. For this reason the total population of Guwahati rose to about 2,22,800 in 1972. The site of capital complex has been selected some road side villages with paddy fields all around near Ganeshguri, Guwahati. Some Assam type building had been constructed at a war footing for the new capital known as Dispur. The decision of shifting the capital of Assam from Shillong to this site was political and administrative and ecological consideration was not taken into account at that time which has now been proved to be an ecological disaster.

Guwahati, today extends nearby 27 km. from the Cantonment area of Satgaon in the east of Khanamukh in the west and about 12 km. from the Brahmaputra in the north to Basisthasram and the National Highway No. 37 in the south. Thus, the city covers an area of 313 sq. km. with the total population of 5,84,342 as per 1991 census.

The present city represents a very low MC* value (7.72) which indicates that Guwahati bears the least resemblance to an ideal shape because of great deviation from circularity. The general shape and size and the plan of the important streets of Guwahati have been influenced by the river flowing to the north on one hand and the hills to the east, south-west and west on the other. The city has been sprawling curvilinear fashion and has roughly a crescent-shape. The recent arterial growth of the city seems to be partly responsible for its lower MC value. Such a spatial shape of Guwahati is a major problem creating obstruction for its ideal morphological growth as

---

* [MC= 100, Aa/3.1416 (Dd/p)2 where MC is the measure of circulariy in shape, Aa is the actual area contained in the urban unit. Dp distance between most distant points on the boundary of the unit.]

well as for planning of the city. The city's morphological expansion has warranted in the multiplicity of locations of public utility centres as well as greater areal expansion of service zones which is no doubt a factor greatly responsible for a slow process in changing the pattern of internal structures of the city relating to beautification and arrangement of such items as roads and buildings which constitute the city's basic elements in morphology. The measure of circularity further gives an indication of the growing linear expansion of the urban structure of Guwahati, thereby accounting for accretion of more of rural areas to its urban jurisdiction and hence, adding diversified elements to the morphology of the city.

The process of urban growth of Guwahati shows a broad zonal and sectoral arrangement from the nucleus to the periphery. In the earlier part of the growth of the city is affected by sets of centripetal forces where Concentric Zone Theory (E. W. Burgess, 1923) and in the later part the Sector Theory (Homer Hoyt, 1939) seems to have operative with some modification consequent upon topographical and cultural barriers. A twin process of outward extension and internal reorganisation is also in operation. The availability of large occupied lands, the presence of transport services and water frontage ensure the possibilities of growth towards the main periphery leading to the sector form of development along the roads. The early settlement clung to the river side and the shape and size of the built up area of the town were governed by the position of the Brahmaputra river and the character of the surrounding hills. The old section of the city is crescent shaped. The water front is on the north and the growth proceeded parallel to the water front streets Guwahati achieved a miximum width opposite the midpoint of the water frontage and indeed in two lateral points resembling the horns of a crescent.

The later development of the city is mainly influenced by cultural factors. Surronding the city core, Guwahati sprawls along the main roads towards the east, south and west. The physical barriers like the hills, marshes and streams lie between the urban appendages. With the shifting of the capital of Assam from Shillong to Guwahati and the tremendous growth of population within the city since independence the marshes are receding and the houses are slowly

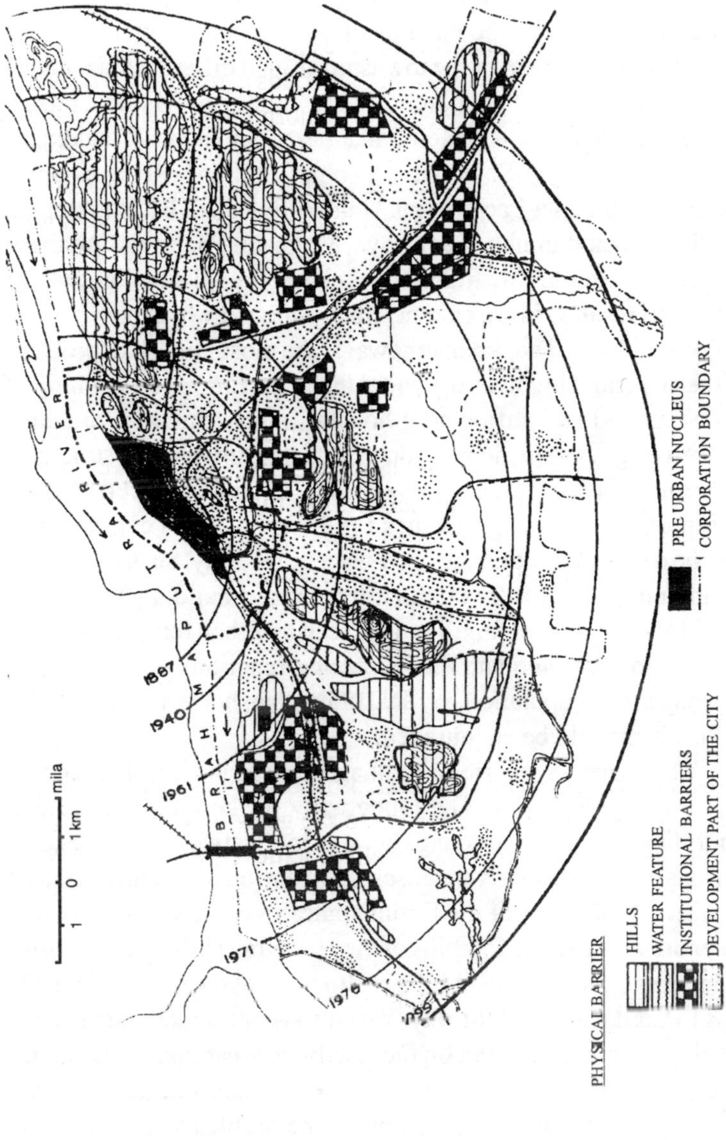

Map 2.1 : Guwahati : Development of concentric & sectoral form

climbing up on the hill slopes. The cultural barriers like the civil lines, Noonmati Oil Refinery, Military Cantonment, enclosures of different factories and mills. Railway colonies, railway stations and other cultural landscape have disturbed the ideal pattern and the irregular development of the township around different axial nuclei appears to have taken place. These nuclei are Fancy bazar-Panbazar-Uzanbazar, Athgaon-Paltanbazar, Silpukhuri-Chandmari-Noonmati, Narangi-Satgaon, Guwahati-Shillong Road, Dispur-Khanapara, Sarania-Lachitnagar, Ulubari-Rehabari, Fatasil-Ambari, Santipur- Bharalumukh, Kamakhya, Maligaon-Pandu and Adabari-Jalukbari-Satmile. The highly irregular and unplanned growth of Guwahati resulted into a chaotic urban situation which pose several major problems. The urban renewal is the most important problem of the city and it involves the widening of narrow roads, opening of the congested and suffocating houses, improvement of drainage and sewerage system, demolition of outdated, dilapidated structures and replacement of these by new houses. A number of well planned and integrated housing schemes for different urban communities may be developed within the open spaces of the city. Such residential communities apart from stimulating a sound building expansion, would also house and families displaced by urban renewal activity. In order to accommodate the increasing functions of the city and growing urban population, vertical rather than horizontal expansion of the city should be encouraged.

The current scenario of drainage system in Guwahati and its environs is quite grim. The topography of the Guwahati region controlling the natural drainage became ineffective during the flood seasons. The Bharalu river causes flood during the summer season because of backflow of the Brahmaputra river. There are no catch water drains along the foothills of the Navagraha hills, Sarania hills, Kalapahar hills, Narakasur hills etc. to prevent the run-off from the hills to habitat areas of the city. Various agencies including private developers, encroachment on the low-lying areas and water bodies together with non-maintenance of the existing drains has made several areas of the city vulnerable to the problems of inundation. The ecology in and around greater Guwahati in totality has now been destroyed by clearing of vegetation, hill cutting for earth and blasting rocks by the vicious circle. It is reported by the Newspapers on July 25, 1999 that faulty policy decisions, rapacious denudation of the forest cover on the hilly areas, indiscriminate cutting of hills and encroachments hills aided and abetted by local politicians have together resulted in the tragic death of ten persons in a major landslide in the Kahilipara colony bazaar hill side area on 24th July, 1999. Similar type of landslides have also been reported from Nabagraha and Kharghuli hills. In order to save the city from the deluge caused by heavy showers, Guwahati needs a futuristic approach for a comprehensive city drainage system. Alarmed by the worsening waterlogging problem faced by Guwahati city, the Assam government recently submitted a Rs. 40 crore drainage project to the Railway Ministry proposing to construct cross drainage network along the railway line stretching from Bharalumukh to Narangi area and also from near the railway station to the river Brahmaputra along with abandoned rail track via Ambari and Uzanbazar. The project when completed is thought to ease the waterlogging problem as the excess water is proposed to be drained out at two ends Bharalumukh and Narangi area. Besides some catch water drains may be constructed along the foothills of the city area to prevent the run-off from the hills from submerging the residential areas of near the hills.

The present road system of Guwahati is not at all convenient. The National Highways 31 and 37, the Assam Trunk Road, the Mahatma Gandhi Road and the G.N. Bordoloi Road are the few major roads contributing to the morphological expansion of the city. The width of these roads is not more than 12 metres and the structural expansion along these roads leads to congestion and hence these are not at all favourable for the high speed traffic. The other roads of the city are short zigzag, very narrow and taking frequent turns in the city. The scope for future development is also very little as the lands on either side of the roads have been encroached upon by other uses. The most of the roads and narrow lanes are not well pitched and have occasional deep spaces which are not conducive to smooth plying of vehicles. Water logging is a common feature seen on the roads during the summer season. Another drawback of the roads is their coating of dust and huge accumulation of filth on them as there is no scientific garbage disposal system. In fact, the conservancy services are as bad as the drainage system in Guwahati. There are few public toilets and urinals in the city and they are not looked after properly. That is why, the foul smell emitted from them is definitely a great hazard to the public health. The other public utility services, such as water supply, electrification, health services, recreational facilities are quite unsatisfactory in the city. Thus, the civic life of the city of Guwahati is by no means comfortable. In order to overcome these problems, a detail survey of the civic needs of the habitants may be worked out and the new proposals like construction of new roads widening existing roads, laying branch sewers on the unsewered roads and lanes, construction of flushed latrines at suitable places may be implemented in phase manner. The above problems of the city cannot be properly solved by the government body alone but could be solved through individual and collective efforts.

References

Brush, John E., "Growth and Spatial Structure of Indian Cities", *Indian Urbanization and Planning: Vehicles of Modernisation,* Allen G Noble and Ashok K. Dutt, Eds. Tata Mcgraw-Hill Publishing Company Limited, New Delhi, 1977, PP. 64-92.

Bhattacharyya, N.N., *Morphology of the Towns of Assam with Special Reference to the City of Gauhati* (An Analytico- Synthetic Study), Mani Manik Press, Gauhati, 1981.

Gibbs, J.P. *Urban Research Methods*, Princeton, 1961. *The Assam Tribune*, Gauhati, July 25,1991.

3

MUNICIPAL SELF-GOVERNMENT IN GUWAHATI AND ITS UTILITY SERVICES

K.M. Deka

Municipal self-government in Guwahati (spelt earlier as Gawhatty and Gauhati) was not a spontaneous development resulting from historical experience. Nor was it introduced by the British Raj so as to educate the 'natives' by acquainting them with the western concept of municipal self-government. The 'natives' living in their 'miserable shanties' (to quote Col. Shakespeare, author of *The History of the Assam Rifles*) there in 'Gawhatty' were opposed to the concept of local self-government as such and were most reluctant to pay municipal taxes. Municipal government was, in fact, forced upon the inhabitants of Gawhatty by the Raj.

The East India Company and also the Crown after 1858 wanted to ensure that civic amenities, including police service, are made available to the local residents in lieu of payment of taxes only. Even in the matter of watch and ward which is a primary function of government, the Governor General-in-Council's considered opinion was as follows:

> The cost of Municipal police ought invariably to be the first charge upon Municipal Fund... Protection of life and property is a primary necessity and cost of police

> maintained expressly for the service of any city of town should, as far as practicable, be defrayed by the inhabitants.[1]

Guwahati despite being the headquarter of the Commissioner of Assam from 1826 to 1871 was notoriously filthy and unhygienic. Not only the stray cattle but the residents as well contributed towards the deterioration of sanitary condition of the town. But there was no law regulating civic affairs, including sanitation. It was in or around 1836 that the Magistrate and the Civil Surgeon took the initiative to form a 'voluntry Town Improvement Committee in Gawhatty'.[2] However, the local residents did neither welcome the idea of municipal self-government nor were they prepared to pay municipal taxes. Therefore, the committee had to depend entirely on government grants for undertaking municipal utilities.

In 1846, the aforesaid Town Improvement Committee made a move to raise a part of its fund from local taxes and so it suggested the levy of a tax on hawkers and traders which the government approved. Two years later, a house tax to be levied in the town was also sanctioned. The so-called voluntary Town Improvement Committee formed by British Officers at Guwahati thus paved the way for the introduction of the Bengal Act XXVI of 1850 in Guwahati which legally consolidated the idea that civic amenities could be had by paying, at least partly, for the utilities. But integration of the local residents into a responsive municipal community could not be forged which was why the necessary co-operation and effective participation in municipal affairs on their part was lacking in the town. That legacy continued.[3]

The Guwahati Municipal Board which was formed in 1853 with the District Magistrate as Chairman and two other English Officials as commissioners has undergone several changes under the subsequent Acts, namely the Acts of 1864, 1876, 1884 (based on the recommendations of the Royal Commission on Decentralisation), 1923 and 1956. The Gauhati Municipal Corporation Act, 1969 was extended to the city in 1974.

The Guwahati Municipal Corporation was constituted with 34 wards in 1974. Since there has been a manifold rise in its population, the ward were delimited and their present strength was fixed at 60. So far three general elections have been held to elect councillors to the Corporation the last one being on 16 May 1995 after a gap of 12 years.

The Corporation has 4 Revenue Zones, 5 PWD Divisions and 23 Public Works Zones, for the convenience of administration. It maintains 1919 roads while the PWD does 237 and the Railways 112 roads, making it to a total of 2268 roads. It may be mentioned that the Corporation has so far handed over 179 roads to the PWD. As regards drains, while all major drains are looked after by the PWD, Government of Assam, 3579 drains, mainly road side ones, are under the charge of the Corporation. The Guwahati Municipal Corporation supplies to certain wards water from three Water Treatment Plants in addition to eight Deep tubewells which together produce about 55 million litres of water daily. The Urban Water Supply and Sewage Board supplies water to the Zoo Road area and the PWD does it to Dispur.

Municipal taxes are never popular in Guwahati. Houses are invariably underrated. Defaults in payment of taxes are numerous; the haves and the have-nots alike are shy; to clear their dues. So the taxes and rates never yield the desired revenue to the Corporation. However, the 4 check gates and 3 parking places of the Guwahati Municipal Corporation generate a major portion of its annual income (Rs. 7.89 crore for 1998-99). The markets numbering eleven are another source of steady income. Besides shared taxes under section 184 of the GMC Act are another important sources of revenue.[4] The total annual income of the GMC from all sources amounts to Rs. 1650.00 lakh of which Rs. 1300.00 lakh are paid as salary to the employees of the Corporation. An amount of Rs. 250.00 lakh is paid to HUDCO by way of repayment of loan. Thus, the Corporation has an amount of Rs. 100.00 lakh only for various services and development works.

II

Physical Growth and Livability

Guwahati expanded both in terms of size and population ever since the formation of the Town Improvement Committee. The town which was lying on both sides of the Brahmaputra comprised an area of four square miles. In 1892, North Gauhati was excluded from the jurisdiction of the Municipal Board whose northern boundary thereafter came to be defined by an imaginary line running through the mid-point of the Brahmaputra. Its size was reduced to 2.95 square miles. Since 1916 Gauhati Municipal Authorities have been pursuing agressive annexation of the outlying areas. In 1939, Kukurmuta (now named Hedyatpur), Rehabari, Shantipur, Sarania and Ulubari were included in the municipal limits. Prior to the constitution of Guwahati into a city, it had an area of ten square miles with 30 municipal wards.

The shifting of the State's capital from Shillong to Guwahati in 1972 saw an abrupt and unprecedented expansion of the city both in areas and population. The capital attracted streams of people from different parts of the state. People of all hues businessmen, land speculators, contractors, construction workers, daily wage earners, rickshaw and thela pullers, job seekers from the villages in lakhs invaded the city thus creating great strain on the never planned–haphazardly grown city. Today Guwahati under its municipal jurisdiction covers an area of 216 square kilometres divided into 60 wards and has a population of 10 lakh.

The agressive incorporation of the vast areas adjoining the old city was not accompanied by appropriate development of civic infrastructure, such as, planned land use, proper roads and drainage, public transit to effectively connect the farflung areas of the oblong city with its main centres of activities and also with each other, housing, sanitation and conservancy, and facilities for physical and mental recreation for inhabitants. All this should have been planned before shifting the capital to Guwahati but was not done. In most of the wards, excepting those in the core city, essential utilities like water supply and conservancy have been left mainly to individual residents themselves to arrange.

Guwahati grew horizontally[5] in the most unplanned manner mainly in size but very little in terms of civic amenities. As a result civic life in the city remains least integrated, the newly annexed areas in particular retaining the aura of their village life. Lacking in essential utilities, having congested drains, and footpaths with uncovered manholes and polluted intolerably by filth and automobile exhaust, Guwahati does not appear to be livable. The beautiful surface of the city has been severly mutilated by encroachment on, and earthcutting from the hills so as to fill up the marshes and lowlying areas which until 1972 served as natural drains of the city. A heavy downpour today wrecks havoc by eroding soil from the topless hills and inundating the whole city. The drains get stuck up with muds, sludge and garbage of all sorts. Landslide claims several human lives every year, besides damaging property. Authorities such as Soil Conservation Department, Antipollution Board, END, PWD, Flood Control Department, Forest Department, GMDA and GMC have been voicing their cancern at the depredation of the city's natural green belt. Several NGOs too have joined this chorus. But nothing concrete has been done to arrest the ongoing onslaught on Guwahati's hills and bills.

The Master Plan for Guwahati, prepared in 1969, was redundant by the shifting of the state's capital to the city. So, another Master Plan was adopted in 1985 which has now been in operation without being updated. It seems that there is not much co-ordination between the GMDA and the GMC. The Commissioner of the GMC admits that it does not deal with the Master Plan excepting in matters of Zoning regulations. Permissions to construct houses and buildings are issued by both the authorities rather too liberally. So, the new localities are growing in a haphazard manner without provisions for proper road and drains as well as open space for parks.

Encroachment on government land in Guwahati is a major problem. Not only low-paid employees and workers and poor migrants in thousands in search of jobs but also land speculators having nexus with high political leaders and bureaucrats are grabbing government land, including reserved land. The GMC used to issue holding numbers to such encroachers on the plea that it generated considerable revenue from house and other municipal taxes levied upon them against their holding numbers. The holding number is a concrete proof of continual occupation of government land on the basis of which settlement with the occupant is made. Besides, the holding number is used for electricity connection, issue of ration cards and even the registration of voters of doubtful citizenship. However, the GMC has stopped issuing holding numbers, rather reluctantly, with effect form 7th May, 1993. Recently it has been stressed that as the GMC alone could not stop encroachment on or evict encroachers from government land, it should resume issuing of holding numbers keeping in view its fund crunch.[7]

It may be noted that government land policies are primarily responsible for large scale encroachment on government land in Guwahati. Sections 14.8 and 14.9 of the Government of Assam Land Policies, 1989 read as follows:

> Suitable land in Guwahati Municipal Corporation area and in other towns may be kept reserved and free from encroachment for construction of Government office/ buildings/institutions etc. *and for other purposes* (emphasis added);
>
> and
>
> Suitable vacant land in Guwahati Municipal Corporation area and in other towns may be kept reserved and free from encroachment for environmental purposes and be handed over to the Municipal Corporation, Municipal Boards and Town Committees.

On the otherhand, section 14.3 of the same Land Policies states that–

> Land within Greater Guwahati notified under Government Notification No. RSR-21/59/126 dated 1st October, 1966 and in any other towns may be settled on payment of due premium

with indigenous persons of the State in order of preference as follows:

(i) An indigenous person who has no land in his name or in the name of any member of his family and *who has been in occupation of Government land with members of his family for last 15 years or more.* (emphasis added)

The Government land policies thus encourage encroachment on government land in the city. Eviction of encroachers is seldom done. Corruption at high levels, at times judicial intervention, human greeds and humanitarian problems stand on the way of protecting government land in Guwahati. So, every inch of government land is facing threats of encroachment. The GMC in a recent general meeting expressed grave concern particularly at encroachment on government reserved land, such as Betkuchi having an area of 366 bighas, not only by ordinary people but also by political leaders and their touts.[8]

The corporation has been urging upon the district authorities to evict all encroachers from the banks of the rivers Bharalu and Bashistha so as to free those natural outlets for drainage, and to stop earthcutting from the hills in order to prevent soil erosion and protect the city's environment. But the response from the district administration is lukewarm for lack of will on the part of its political masters. Thus, depredation of government land is one of the most serious obstacles in the path of development of Guwahati in a planned way.

III

Public Utilities in Guwahati : An overview

Municipal utilities are grouped into two broad categories– (i) Productive Services and (ii) Environmental services. The first category may be roughly defined as those services if availed of by an individul would mean a charge on him and so the maintenance of such services yields revenue to the municipal authority. Also democratic viability in relation to the administration and management of these services by a municipal body distinguishes it from private business. Thus the utilitarian philosophy is underlying the concept of municipal utilities throughout the globe. Even in the United States of America the public utilities are provided by the municipal corporations at a comparatively much cheaper price,[9] and therefore these have through centuries remained the major domain of the government at the grassroot level.

A comprehensive list of utilities is not possible, for, laws differ from country to country. However, water supply and conservancy are the two utilities which are administered by the local authorities throughout the world. The Guwahati Municipal Board used to undertake these two 'Public Utility Services' under various Municipal Acts. Its successor, the Guwahati Municipal Corporation too provides these services now called 'essential services'[10] to the Guwahatians.

Environmental services are intended to promote the general welfare of the community. Their benefits are derived by the residents of the city, no matter wheather they pay any tax to the corporation or not. However, the corporation expects not only financial contribution in the form of certain general taxes but concerted efforts and co-operation from the city dwellers as well. This expectation is manifest in the municipal laws. For instance, a municipal body needs unfailing cooperation from the inhabitants in such matters as sanitation, control of communicable diseases, vaccination, inoculation, regulation of food items, vital statistics etc. The following were some of the environmental services undertaken by the Guwahati Municipal Board : police, communication (including ferry services), hospital and medical services, vaccination, drainage, registration of births and deaths, education, public parks, libraries and halls etc. However, police and ferry services do not any longer figure in the list of functions of the GMC. Education too has now become an insignificant subject of the Corporation. It maintains only six schools of which five are primary schools and one high school.

Essential services of the Guwahati Municipal Corporation are discussed below.

IV

Water Supply

Historical background : Protected water is the basic requirement for health of the people. The problems faced by municipal authorities in administering this service are gigantic. In addition to the major problem of funds, there are other problems such as availability of good water sources, pollution control, and efficient sewerage system, to mention only a few of them which have tremendous brearing upon the water supply scheme of a municipal body. Guwahati is indeed fortunate to have the Brahmaputra as the exhaustible surface source of water which the Corporation uses for supplying treated water to certain wards of the city. In addition, the GMC has been exploiting its ground water.

Guwahati Municipal Board during the first three decades of its existence (1853-1883) did not supply water to the residents. It was in October 1883 that the Board had applied to the Government for a loan of Rs. 38000 for construction of a water plant which was readily sanctioned.[11] But the amount was inadequate. So, the Chief Commissioner of Assam (Elliot) decided to take up the project as a provincial one despite contrary policy of the Government of India. The project was executed by the PWD of Assam. On 1 June, 1887, the water works was handed over to the Guwahati Municipal Board. It was designed to supply 100 litres of water per head per day. After two years it was found that water source of the plant was constantly polluted. So, the barge was removed upstream of the River. In 1892, the plant broke down twice. Next year it was thoroughly repaired by the Provincial Government and was handed over to the PWD on the condition that the cost of its operation would be borne by the Municipal Board.[12] The great earthquake of 1897 wrecked havoc in Guwahati and damaged its water works. It was repaired at a cost of Rs. 10,000 by the Provincial Government and operated by the PWD until 1925.

The water works was handed over to the Municipal Board in 1925 together with an assurance that liberal loan would be sanctioned to it for execution of a new water supply scheme. The estimated cost of the project was Rs. 109,628. However, it was raised to Rs. 283,639. The promised loan was not sanctioned by the government. So, the Board adopted a five year plan in 1933 to improve the existing plant, the cost of which was borne by itself. In 1958, the Board contracted a Union Government loan of Rs. 105 lakh to implement a comprehensive water works scheme for Guwahati. The new plant was completed in 1962-63 and it was expected to supply 103.5 lakh gallons of water per day, calculated at the rate of 8 gallons per head per day, being the quantity of water supplied since 1887.[13] Besides, the distribution of water as seen from record was never equitable; certain wards were served liberally while others received only scanty supply. As to its quality, it was not always above suspicion. The Director of Public Health in his Inspection Report wrote, for instance that the filtration is too rapid to yield satisfactory and dependable water.

From a quick look at the history of water supply scheme in Guwahati it appears that (i) the municipal authority in Guwahati suffered from fiscal disabilities in providing protected water to the residents; (ii) therefore, the Provincial (State) and the Union Government were involved in funding the water works, and at times in managing the service; (iii) the quantity of water was in average 20 litres per head per day which was too inadequate; (iv) distribution of water was not judicious and (v) quality of water supplied was not always commendable. These legacies have continued ever after the Municipal Board of Guwahati was succeeded by the Guwahati Municipal Corporation.

At present there are three major authorities which supply protected water to the inhabitants of Guwahati. Those are the GMC, Urban Water Supply and Sewage Board, and the Public Works Department (Government of Assam). Besides, the Gauhati Refinery and the NF Railways have their own water supply schemes. While the GMC serves the core city, the UWS & S Board serves the Zoo Road area and the PWD operates its water supply scheme for Dispur.

The water supply scheme at Pan Bazar set up by the Guwahati Municipal Board in 1960 has been overhauled during

1992-97 and its capacity increased. The other plants installed at Satpukhuri and Kamakhya were likewise expanded. Besides, a dozen Deep Tubewells have been installed in areas not covered by the present water supply schemes. The following table shows the installed capacity of the present water works under the GMC:

Table-3.1 : Installed capacity of the existing water works schemes under the GMC

Name of the Scheme	Water produced (in million litres per day)
Pan Bazar Plant	45.00
Satpukhuri Plant	27.50
Kamakhya Plant	4.70
Deep Tubewells & Spot Source Scheme	7.80
Total Capacity	: 80.00 million litres per day
Total actual production	: 55.40 MLD.

Whereas, tap connections are provided from the Pan Bazar and Satpukhuri Plants, only Street taps are provided from the Kamakhya Plant and the DT Schemes, excepting in New Field, Shantipur and certain areas of Bharalumukh. It should also be noted that water supplied from the DT Scheme is not treated and hence its quality is anybody's guess.

Service areas under various plants of water supply in the city are shown in Table 3.2.

The water supply schemes operated by various authorities produce a total quantity of 90 million litres of water per day. The Corporation's water supply plants serve hardly 4,00,000 inhabitants out of a total population of 10,00,000. The other schemes cover only a few of the remaining areas which were brought under the jurisdiction of the corporation after 1974. While the well-to-do sections of these people have arranged their own water supply by installing deep tube-wells, the poor masses depend on ring wells, kachha wells and natural sources like the Khanabil, the River and its rivulets. The Corporation collects water tax from every holding. Therefore, there is tremendous pressure upon it for supply of protected water.

Table 3.2 : Service area under the existing water supply schemes of the GMC

Name of the Plant	Areas Served
A. *Pan Bazar Plant*	
(i) Reservoir at DC's residence	Pan Bazar, Lakhtakia, Kamarpatty Fancy Bazar (part), Machkhowa, Kumarpara, Athgaon, Tokobari.
(ii) Sarania Hill Reservoir	Dhakin Sarania, Pubsarania, Gandhi Basti, Ulubari, Rehabari, Manipuri Basti.
(iii) Direct Pumping	Part of Fancy Bazar, Sukleswar, Satrakar, Professor Colony of Cotton College, Uzaan Bazar (part).
B. *Satpukhuri Plant*	
(i) Reservoir at Housing Colony	Karnachal, Nizorapar, Nabagraha, (plains), Milanpur, Krishnanagar Housing Colony.
(ii) Nabagraha	Nabagraha hills, Golakdham, Happy Villa, Chenikuthi (plain).
(iii) Chitrachal	Chitrachal, Nabagraha (part), Cheni kuthi (part).
(iv) Satpukhuri hillock	Uzan Bazar, Guwahati Club area, Silpukhuri, Chandmari, Bamunimaidan, Rajgarh (part), Pubsarania, Karnachal (part), Kharghuli (hill), Upper Strand Road, Chenikuthi (hill), Hilly part of Chandmari.
(v) Direct Pumping	Kharghuli (part) and Bankonwar Nagar.
C. *Kamakhya Plant*	
(i) Reservoir at Bhubeneswari	Kamakhya and Bhubaneswari temple areas through 79 street taps.

The Table 3.3 shows the areas served by the Deep Tubewell Scheme of the GMC.

As per WHO norms a person needs minimum of 135 litres of protected water per day. The quantity of water consumption in the USA is far above 450 litres per head per day. Guwahati needs about 156 million litres of water to serve its population but the existing water works produce only 90 million litres of water daily thus leaving a gap of 66 million litres between the demand for water and its actual supply. Apparently keeping this gap in view

Table 3.3 : Deep Tubewell Scheme under GMC and its areas of operation.

Place of installation		Areas Served
1.	Barsapara	Rang Pathar, AK Deb Path, Gopal Mandir (part), Tula Factory, Dilip Hazari Path, Mayurkrishna Cinema area.
2.	Fatasil Harizon Colony	Fatasil Bazar, Gopal Mandir (part), Harizon Colony, New Bisnupur Puja Mandap.
3.	Bharalumukh	B.R.P. Road, New Harizon Bhawan area, Goenka N.H. area, G.S. Colony, Ambari.
4.	Shantipur	Shantipur (part), Bhutnath, Durga Sarobar, Kalipur.
5.	New Field	Paltan Bazar (part), Chatribari (part), Nepali Mandir, Rehabari (part), Sabipur, Bilpar.
6.	Gopinath Nagar	Shankarpur (hill), Birubari market.
7.	Kalapahar	Birubari (part)
8.	Garigaon	Garigaon area.

the GMC has proposed a new water supply scheme. The execution of the scheme would cost Rs. 444 crore. The Corporation approached the UNESCO for necessary fund but the latter sanctioned an amount of Rs. 120 crore only. Therefore, a loan of Rs. 239 crore has been contracted with HUDCO and the project accordingly trimmed. The intake point of the proposed project will be set up at Kharghuli and the treatment plant at Ramcha hill. When implemented, the scheme will be able to supply water to six lakh residents living in Chandmari, Bamunimaidan, Zoo Road, Ganeshguri, Dispur, Hatingaon and Khanapara areas of the city.[14]

It is evident that the proposed water supply scheme will serve areas which have been receiving water from the existing schemes already. On the other hand, west Guwahati has been continually neglected since inception of the Corporation in matters of civic utilities. Several councillors have come out heavily against the discriminatory treatment of west Guwahati by the Corporation and demanded that west Guwahati where several areas are no better than slums should be covered by the new water works proposed to be implemented by the Corporation. It was highlighted by several councilors that in the hilly areas in west Guwahati no tubewell or ring well can be dug for obvious reasons and as a result residents there in these localities have to depend on the River.[15] Nothing concrete excepting a vague assurance that all wards numbering from 1 to 60 would be covered by the new project when necessary funds from UNESCO and HUDCO are received.

The failure of the GMC to fully exploit the Brahmaputra as the sole water source and to supply adequate treated water to the residents has created another serious problems in the city. Not only the water supply authorities of the city have exploited ground water by installing deep tubewells but also private developers of high rise housing apartments which today criss-cross not only the core but several developing areas of the city as well are engaged in wanton exploitation of ground water. It is being done in the most unplanned and unscientific manner thereby causing alarming depletion in the ground water level of the city. It has been noticed that in certain areas the level of depletion is as high as 4.45 metres.[16] A survey of the possible ground water levels by remote sensing satellite has been done to identify the existing ground water beds of the city which unfortunately are not many.[17]

There is no provision in the Gauhati Municipal Corporation Act or any other existing laws regulating the use of ground water. Therefore, no permission from the Corporation is required for installing deep tubewells by residents and the real estate developers. Even judicial action at the level of the Supreme Court has not yet resulted in the formulation of uniform laws throughout the country for planned and judicious exploitation of ground water.[18]

The magnitude of wanton exploitation of ground water can be appreciated if one looks at the experience of Kolkata. A recent survey by the Central Ground Water Authority has revealed an alarming drop in ground water levels in Kolkata and the fall is between 5 to 9 metres. This depletion in ground water level together with the heavy weight of the high rise buildings in the areas covered by the aforesaid survey may cause a severe subsidence of surface soil and consequently a vast area of Kolkata may sink.[19]

Unless judicious and scientifically planned exploition of ground water is resorted Guwahati also may sooner or later, face the threat of subsidence. Therefore, proper planning and rigorous regulations are needed to use the City's ground water so as to conserve this resource and to protect Guwahati from potential subsidence.

V

Conservancy in Guwahati

Maintenance of sanitation involves the disposal of sewage, general conservancy and surface cleanliness. Conservancy is one of the oldest charges of the Guwahati Municipal Board. Since 1856, conservancy has been the greatest challenge to the city which could hardly be met effectively due mainly to paucity of funds and habits of the inhabitants. So, the Commissioner of Assam in his letter to the Governmant of Bengal, dated 29 November 1865, stressed the need to treat conservancy as a provincial subject instead of being classified as a municipal one.[20] But it was not accepted by the government. So, the entire resource of the Guwahati Municipal Board for a long time was employed in the maintenance of general conservancy although with a little success. The Guwahati Municipal Corporation's record in this respect is no better than that of its predecessor. Indiscriminate use of non-degradable polythene papers and bags made thereof has further aggravated the chronic insanitary condition of the city.

Conservancy arrangement made first by the Guwahati Municipal Board in 1863 consisted of 2 carts, 2 bullocks, 2 cart drivers and 6 'coolies'. In 1939 it comprised a Health Officer, 20 rubbish porters, 20 road sweepers, 17 bullocks, 20 carts, 2 wheel barrows and 5 ponnies. In 1962, 5 tractors, 4 trucks and 335 sweepers were engaged to remove garbages from the town and dump them in the Fatasil trenching ground, the only one in the town after the Sarania trenching ground was closed around the year 1960. The method of garbage disposal was open and untreated.

Under the Guwahati Municipal Corporation, conservancy services are under direct supervision of the Corporation's PWD staff. Garbages thrown into the drains and around the dustbins (where those are provided by the Corporation) and on the streets as well as other spoils retrieved from the drains are collected and dumped untreated at the Barsapara trenching ground. Recently a trenching ground each at Amingaon, Lokhra, Khanapara and Chandrapur has been proposed by the GMC. If the proposal is implemented, then the city will be organised into four conservancy circles for disposal of garbage.[21] In the meanwhile a new development took place. The GMC has decided to privatize garbage collection on no payment basis by either party and recently a signed MoU with a Kolkata firm which will use the city's garbage as raw material for power generation. The company shall require 400 metric tons of garbage daily for its plant but Guwahati generates about 200 metric tons only. So, the viability of the project which is expected to commence from April 2000 is doubtful. Besides, the company will remove only such garbage which could be used for power generation thus leaving mud and sludge on the roads as over before. So, even after the project takes off, the conservancy problem shall remain though not as acute as it is now. However, the problem created by plastic and polythene may be partially solved. The success of the project will also depend on the co-operation of the residents inas much as the garbage generated in each household will have to be deposited at fixed points which will be collected daily by the company.

As mentioned already the GMC shall not receive any revenue from the firm for the city's garbage used for generation of electricity. The Corporation, however, has insisted on a security of Rs. 500,000.00 from the contracting firm before starting work on the project.[22] It is understood that the Government will allot the required land to the Company near Dispur for installation of its plant.

The Guwahati Municipal Corporation has also discussed ways and means for solid waste management in the city, keeping in view an interim report of a committee of the Supreme Court. But, the Corporation postponed the creation of separate Conservancy

Department in view of the fact that the final report of the said committee submitted to the Supreme Court was yet to be heard and disposed of. Besides, it was argued by several councillors that the proposal on solid waste management as prepared by the Suprintending Engineer of Conservancy dealt mainly with the creation of separate Department,[23] by bifurcating the present Public Works Department of the GMC. Earlier, a five year project in regard to conservancy had been adopted by the Corporation which was awaiting approval of the State Government. It was, therefore, decided that the proposal submitted by the Superintending Engineer conservancy should be referred to the Standing Committee on Public Health and Water Supply before taking it up in another meeting of the GMC.

Thus, conservancy service in Guwahati is still managed in the most primitive manner. The Corporation engages 21 trucks, including 5 of its own, of which 4 to 5 vehicles do not turn up daily for duty. At present it engages 5 escavators and 12 tippers hired for Rs. 80000.00 per day. But the mud and sludge collected form drains are not removed immediately from the roads although the GMC has 1234 regular and 621 casual labourers mostly engaged in sanitation of the city and those filths are swept again into the drains. Thus, one finds the drains filled with garbage of all sorts and those are, therefore, suffering from acute stagnation.

Citizens' habit of throwing garbage on the roads and into the drains has not much changed over the last 163 years or so of Guwahati's urban life. The hotels, restaurants, nursing homes and hospitals of the city are also to be blamed for worsening Guwahati's sanitation. The GMC has not been able to provide adequate number of dustbins in which garbages and household refuses are supposed to be deposited. Recently, the Mayor of Guwahati moved a proposal for imposition of heavy penalty upon recalcitrant citizens which the general meeting of the GMC adopted on 28-6-1999. The penalty was fixed at Rs. 150.00 for every offence relating to sanitation of the city.

While extending support to the Mayor's proposal, several councillors stressed the need for civic education. Such an educative programmes was undertaken in the meanwhile in which the Governor of Assam also participated but its impact on the Guwahatians may not be much. Therefore, penal measures should be taken against those who habitually pollute the city. In this respect, Guwahati may follow the practice of Delhi and the sanitary staff may be empowered to take action on the spot by issuing challans to the guilty residents. Of course, the Corporation must first of all set an example through its own action that it really means to keep the city free of garbages. Right now neither the GMC nor the people of Guwahati seem concerned at the horrible insanitary condition of the city. In 1926, the Director of Public Health, Government of Assam, made the following observation in his inspection report on the Gauhati Municipal Board:

> Nothing has been done since my inspection in 1924 to improve the disgraceful and most insanitary condition of the roadside drains. I have never seen any drains in this province that are so wantonly neglected. Every imaginable form of filth is being deposited or swept or washed into these drains with the result that they are not only nuisance from the stench which emanates from them but also are positive source of grave danger to the inhabitants of the town.

Were he to reinspect Guwahati today, he would most probably use stronger words than those chosen by him in 1926. Neither the GMC nor the inhabitants of the city can object to such condemnation.

VI

Summing Up

From the foregoing discussion it appears that civic infrastructure and public utility services are not adequate in Guwahati, particularly after 1972. Ever since, the state's capital shifted from Shillong to Guwahati, the city has been growing physically in an unprecedented scale; its population has increased ten fold and its territorial area has expanded about fourteen times. But its physical growth has not been accompanied by corresponding expansion and improved efficiencies in the provision of civic amenities, particularly conservancy and water supply. Guwahati's liability largely depends on efficient management of this public utilities. As at present, the Gauhati Municipal Corporation has not succeeded in managing them efficiently. Logically, therefore, Guwahati should shrink considerably but for scarcities of all sorts which the city's ever-increasing population do have in abundence. Likewise, de-annexation of the outlying areas of the city would also not be a viable proposition, for, politicians and people alike would oppose it. So, Guwahati would continue to grow *sans* adequate civic amenities even in first century of the coming millennium.

Footnotes

1. The Governor General-in-Council contended that police system in India was strictly municipal. The Commissioner of Assam disputed this view but he too was in favour of the transfer of police system to Municipal Board so that "the menace of loose and diseased horses could be effectively dealt with". (vide proceedings of Gauhati Municipal Board, date 17-11-1866).
2. V. Venkata Rao, 'Beginning of Local Self-Government in Assam' in *Journal of Gauhati University* (Arts) , Vol. XIV, 1963.
3. The inhabitants of Guwahati are used to throw rubbish and of fensive materials on roads and into the drains. The menace continued to be discussed frequently by the Municipal authority. Penal measures are also taken against the offenders but the habits of Guwahatians remain unchanged. (Vide proceedings of the Gauhati Municipal Board, 26-8-1863 and that of the GMC, 28-6-1999.)
4. Proceeds of Land Revenue, Local Rates, Property Tax, Motor Vehicle Tax and Entertainment Tax collected in Guwahati, reduced by the collection charges, are to be paid to the GMC.
5. The term 'horizontal' has been used in its ordinary sense and not to be confused with the concepts of 'horizontal' and 'vertical' city. For a discussion on these concepts, see W. Rybczynski & P. D. Linneman, 'How to Save Our shrinking cities' in *The Public Interest*, U.S.A. Inc, Spring 1999, pp. 30-44.
6. GMC spends every year an amount of Rs. 130,000.00 per ward under head 'FDR' (Flood Damage Repair). Vide proceedings of the General Meeting of GMC, 27-5-1998.

7. Proceedings of General Meeting of GMC, 16-8-1995.
8. Some GMC Councillors mentioned specifically the encroachment of Reserved Land at Betkuchi by political leaders and other persons. (Vide Proceedings of General Meeting, GMC, 25-9-95).
9. Vide GMC Act, 1969, Sec. 26.
10. G. B. Hathorn, H. R. Penniman & M. F. Ferber, *Government and Politics in the United States*, D. Van Nostrand & Co. Ltd, Princeton, 1965, p. 752.
11. Proceedings Home-A, 1883, No. 153, p. 12.
12. *Annual Municipal Report*, Govt. of Assam, 1895-96.
13. V. Venkata Rao, *A hundred years of Local Self-Government in Assam*, Bani Prakash, Guwahati, 1963, p. 349.
14. Vide Proceedings of Gauhati Municipal Corporation's General Meeting, 28-6-1999.
15. *Ibid.*
16. Arpan Datta, 'Jal Aharanar Nischit aru Niyantrit Anchanir Ab[illegible]kata' in *Prantik*, 16-31 January, 1999, pp. 18-20.
17. *The Assam Tribune*, Guwahati, 1-9-96.
18. Arpan Datta, *op. cit.*
19. *The Times of India*, New Delhi, 23-9-99, p.1.
20. Vide Letter No. 19J, 29-11-1865. He observed, 'It would be absurd in the present state of affairs to treat these matters as essentially local and municipal'.
21. Proceedings of General Meeting, GMC, 25-9-95.
22. These information have been collected from Chief Engineer, Public Works Department of GMC.
23. As per the proposal, the Conservancy Department shall have one Superintending Engineer, 4 Asstt. Engineers, 2 Junior Engineers, 2 Sanitary Inspectors and 8 Inspectors to supervise works of the sweepers, road and conservancy labourers.

4

WATER SUPPLY IN GREATER GUWAHATI
Problems and Prospects

H. Nath, D. Bhattacharjee & S. Bezbaruah

1. INTRODUCTION

1.1. *General*

It is our common experience that a city dweller in Guwahati has to confront a number of problems in his daily life, e.g. storm water drainage, scarcity of drinking water, traffic congestion, air and water pollution and garbage disposal etc. Of these next to air, water is most vital for human survival. It is a paradox that a city like Guwahati situated on the bank of mighty river Brahmaputra suffers from glaring problem of water scarcity. This is a long persisted fact. It existed even in 50 year back and still it is continuing.

Guwahati became a Municipal town in the year 1865 and this was declared a city in 1974. Rapid development after independence, specially in the field of education, commerce, roads and railway communication brought rapid growth of population and unplanned expansion of Guwahati along with various civic problems.

The population of Guwahati which was hardly 8394 in 1891 became 5,84,342 in 1991 as per census. Municipal area which was

7.86 sq. km in 1951 is now 216.19 sq. km. under Guwahati Municipal Corporation (G.M.C.). Present trend in growth of population in Guwahati is shown in Fig. 4.1.

1.2 *Basic Data*

1.2.1 *Physical Feature*

Guwahati City is situated on the southern bank of the River Brahmaputra. Khasi Hill is on its south and east, low land area with Deepar beel is on the west. On the north, lies North Guwahati, Agiathuri Hills etc. There are some major streams flowing through the city and functioning as natural, storm water drainage channel. These are 'Bharalu', Basistha Bahini, Mara Bharalu and Khajan river which finally end in River Brahmaputra.

There are several hillocks within the valley forming part of city's natural feature. The main hillocks are at Kharghuli, Ramsa, Japorigog, Nilachal, Kamakhya, Kalapahar, Narakasur and Fatasil.

The average elevation of the plain area of the valley varies between 49 to 51 m above M.S.L. whereas, maximum elevation of hillock is around 309 m.

1.2.2 *Climate and Rainfall*

The climate of the city is tropical in nature with three distinct seasons, *viz.* summer, monosoon and winter. Winter is of short duration.

Average annual rainfall of Guwahati is 1637.3 mm and 90% of this occurs between April to September and maximum rainfall period is July to August.

Average temperature varies between 12°C to 32°C with lowest temperature being 10°C and highest to 39°C.

1.2.3 *Geology*

Guwahati and its surrounding area has two distinct geological formations –the alluvial plain of Brahmaputra interrupted by gneisses and schists. It also has marshy tracts and valley fill areas. Broad classification of a typical soil profile (excluding hills) is as follows:

(1) Top layer containing river deposition of medium to fine

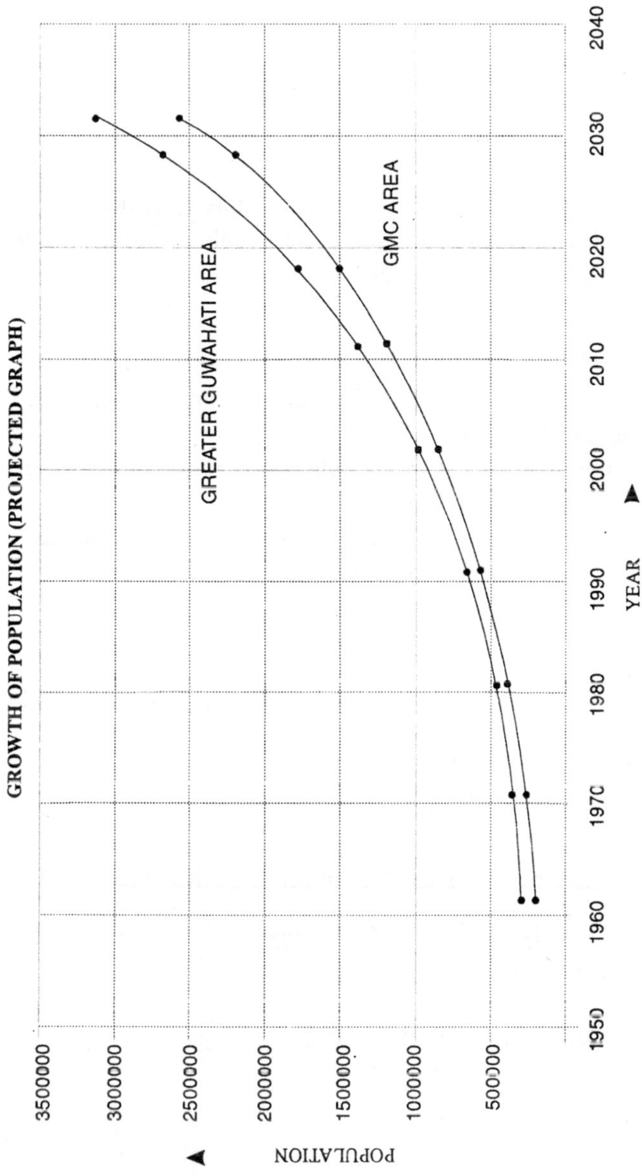

Fig. 4.1 : Growth of Population (Projected Graph)

silt which varies in thickness from place to place and on an average extends to 10 m below ground level. It is often mixed with deposited vegetation and other organic matters.

(2) Next layer/strata extends to a depth of about 25 to 30 m below ground level. This has medium to fine sandy silt/ silty sand with occasional clay pockets.

(3) Below this, lies dense to coarse sand with occasional pebbles or cobbes upto about 45 m below round surface and there is no evidence of rock formation within this zone.

Hydrogeological investigation reveals that within greater Guwahati–

(a) Low duty D.T.W. is feasible in some areas where yield may be $<30\ m^3/h$.

(b) Medium duty D.T.W. is feasible in very limited areas where yield may be 30-100 m^3/h.

(c) Heavy duty D.T.W. is feasible in Borhar, Azara, Dharapur area. Yield $> 100\ m^3/h$.

A map of ground water source in greater Guwahati is indicated in ANNEXURE -1.

2. PRESENT STATUS OF WATER SUPPLY UNDER GMC AREA

2.1 Greater Guwahati can be divided into two parts :

(i) Guwahati Municipal Corporation area.

(ii) Fringe or periurban area bordering GMC area.

GMC is served partly by piped water supply system covering about 40% of its area whereas city dwellers in remaining areas depend partly on GMC deep tube wells, and IM-II, IM-III hand pumps and/or private Ring wells and shallow hand pumps.

2.2 The City supply is inadequate in respect of quantity and sometimes quality. Sub-surface water collected from shallow tube wells, ring wells are very poor in quality as water of these sources are contaminated with faecal coliform and that too dry up during dry period of year.

A sample water analysis report given in Table 4.1A will indicate the status.

Table 4.1A : Typical Water Analysis Report for Spot Sources

Source : Ring Well Solapar, Paltan bazar		Source : D.T.W. Basisthapur, Dispur		Source : D.T.W. Barthakur Mill Road, Ulubari Physical Characteristics:	
pH	6.3	pH	7.2	pH	6.8
Total Solids	704 mg/l	Turbidity Colour	30 N.T.U. Brown	Turbidity	50 N.T.U.
Total Hardness as $CaCO_3$	484 mg/l	Total Solids	264mg/l	Chemcical characteristics (mg/l)	
Chloride	150 mg/l	Total hardness	162mg/l	Total Solids	482
Amm. Nitrogen	0.09 mg/l	Total Iron	1.3 mg/l	T. Hardness $CaCO_3$	260
Alb Nitrogen	0.08 mg/l	Chloride	16 mg/l	Carbonate Hardness $CaCO_3$	260
		Amm. Nitrogen	0.24mg/l	M. Alk as $CaCO_3$	358
		Alt Nitrogen	0.06 mg/l	P-Alk as $CaCO_3$	Nil
Bacteriological Characteristics				Calcium as $CaCO_3$	144
	MPN/100 ml			Magnesium Mg	116
Coliforn organisms	2400		Nil	Iron as Fe	5.00
E. Coli	1100		Nil	Manganese	0.13
Date/Year	16-2-99	24-5-99		Arsenic	Nil
				Chloride as Cl	38.0
				Sulphate as SO_4	30.00
				Nitrate as NO_3	0.36
				Fluoride	Nil
				Amm Nitrogen	0.08
				Alb Nitrogen	0.02
				Bacteriological Char.	
					MPN/100 ml
				Coliform organisms	Nil
				E.Coli	Nil
				Date of Coll.	23-3-98

Table 4.1B : Recent Bacteriological Water Analysis Report of Existing Intake Sites (1999) (River Brahmaputra)

Date	Location	Coliform Organisms MPN/100 ml	E.Coli MPN/100 ml
15-09-1998	Satpukhuri	24,000	4,300
22-09-1998	Kharguli	110,000	46,000
15-09-1998	Panbazar	46,000	9,300
14-09-1998	Kamakhya	240,000	110,000
14-09-1998	Siva Mandir (Pandughat)	460,000	240,000

2.3 At present three agencies, *viz.* GMC,PHED[1], AUWS & SB[2] supply water to different areas of the city. Apart from these three, there are two Central Government establishment, namely Guwahati Refinery (IOC) and NE Frontier Railway (NFR) who have their own independent water supply schemes (within Greater Guwahati) and supply water to their employees only.

The other establishments like OIL and Defence occupying a large part of Satgaon area have independent distribution systems which are fed by water from IOC Treatment Plant (TP) under a mutual agreement between them though supply is inadequate to meet the demand.

Total quantity of water produced and distributed by GMC, PHED and AUW and SB is about 83.50 Mld out of which 79.00 Mld is produced in different TPs from surface sources and balance 4.50 Mld is supplemented by water from deep tube wells (DTW), IM II/III, and shallow hand pumps installed by GMC. The details of production from different installations, and area served are roughly shown in Table 4.2.

1. Public Health Engineering Department, Government of Assam.
2. Assam Urban Water Supply and Sewerage Board.

Table 4.1C : Raw Water Quality of River Brahmaputra

Sl No.	Physical Characteristics	Sample-I	Sample-II	Sample-III	Sample-IV	Sample-V	Sample-VI
1	Appearance	Turbid	Turbid	Turbid	Turbid	Turbid	Turbid
2	Turbidity (NTU)	100	70	90	75	100	
3	pH	7.7	7.7	7.8	7.8	7.6	
Chemical Characteristics (mg/1)							
4	Total Solids	140	150	160	150	168	
5	Suspended Solids	106	114	126	114	132	
6	Total Hardness as $CaCO_3$	90	92	94	92	92	
7	Carbonate Hardness as $CaCO_3$	74	76	82	76	74	
8	P. Alkalinity as $CaCO_3$	Nil	Nil	Nil	Nil	Nil	
9	M. Alkalinity as $CaCO_3$	74	76	82	76	74	
10	Calcium as Ca	24	24.8	28	25.6	24.8	
11	Magnesium as Mg	7.2	7.2	5.76	6.24	7.2	
12	Iron as Fe	1.7	0.56	0.8	0.94	0.54	
13	Manganese as Mn	Nil	Nil	Nil	Nil	Nil	
14	Chloride as Cl	4.0	2.0	3.0	Nil	Nil	
15	Sulphate as SO_4	18.0	15.0	12	20.0	16.0	
16	Fluoride as F	Trace	Trace	Trace	Trace	Trace	

(Contd.)

Table 4.1C : (Contd.)

17	Filtrate as NO_3	Trace	Nil	Trace	Trace	Trace
18	Amm. Nitrogen as NH_3	0.02	0.01	0.01	0.01	0.02
19	Alb. Nitrogen as NH_3	0.01	0.01	0.01	0.01	0.01
Bacteriological Characteristics						
	Coliform Organisms. MPN/100 ml	46,000	11,000	460,000	46,000	1,100,000
	E. Coli organisms MPN/100ml	24,000	21,000	240,000	9,300	460,000
	Date of Collection	5-11-97	5-11-97	5-11-97	5-11-97	5-11-97
	Place of Collection (Intake site)	Satpukhuri (Kharguli)	Panbazar	Kamakhya	Pandughat	Sadilapur

Table 4.2 : Different Installations and Production of Water

Sl. No.		Location of T.P./P.H	Year of expiry of design life	Source of water	Intake	Treatment Process	Present production	Installed capacity	Zone/area served
1	2	3	4	5	6	7	8	9	10
A. Surface Sources (GMC)									
1	GMC T.P (1960)	Panbazar	1980	R. Brahmapura Panbazar	Barge	Conventional	34.00	45.00 (10Mgd)	Panbazar, Fancy bazar, Kumarpara, Atgaon, Paltan bazar, Ulubari Sarania, Lachit-nagar.
2.	PHED T.P. (1975)	Panbazar	2006	R. Brahmapura Panbazar	Barge	Conventional	11.25	11.25 (2.5Mgd)	Medical College, Dispur, AAU, Henigrabari etc.
3.	GMC T.P. (1985)	Satpukhuri	2000	R. Brahmapura	Barge Kharguli	Conventional	18.00	22.50 (5Mgd)	
4.	AUWS&SB T.P. (1995)	Hengrabari	2010	R. Brahmapura	Barge Kharguli	Conventional	11.25	11.25 (2.5Mgd)	Zoo Rd., Hengrabari Japrigog
5.	(i) Kamakhya (Old) GMC T.P (1956)	Kamakhya Hill (foot hill)	1986	R.Brahmapura	Direct pumping	Sedimentation only	0.25	1.35 (0.3Mgd)	Kamakhya Hill
	(ii) New Kamakhya GMCT.P. (1992)	Kamakhya Hill	2007	R.Brahmapura	Barge near Kalipur Asram	Conventional	Not in operation	4.50 (1Mgd)	Kamakhya Hill Town

Table 4.2 (Contd.)

1	2	3	4	5	6	7	8	9	10
6.	PHED T.P (Julukbari) (1970-71)	University Jalukbari	2001	R.Brahmapura	Barge near Pandu	Conventional	4.50	4.50 (1Mgd)	Guwahati University, Engg. College, Ayurvedic College
B. Ground Water (GMC and PHED)									
7.	D.T.W	New Field	–	Ground Water	Direct pumping	No treatment	0.35	–	Satribari, Rehabari and others
8.	D.T.W	Gopinath Nagar	–	Ground Water	Direct pumping	No treament	0.36	–	Birubari, Kalapahar and others
9.	D.T.W	Fatasil	–	Ground Water	Direct pumping	No treament	0.35	–	Fatasil
10.	D.T.W	T. Phukan Park	–	Ground Water	Direct pumping	No treatment	0.15	–	Fatasil
11.	D.T.W	Rangpathar	–	Ground Water	Direct pumping	No treatnent	0.16	–	Ambari, Tinali Dhirenpara
12.	D.T.W	Barsapara	–	Ground Water	Direct pumping	No treatnent	0.15	–	Odalbakhra, Kahilipara
13.	D.T.W	Kalapahar	–	Ground Water	Direct pumping	No treatment	0.20	–	Kalapahar main Rd., Cycle factory area
14.	D.T.W	Santipur	–	Ground Water	Direct pumping	No treatment	0.20	–	Santipur, Durga Sarovar

Table 4.2 *(Contd.)*

1	2	3	4	5	6	7	8	9	10
15.	D.T.W	Sarusajai	–	Ground Water	Direct pumping	No treatment	0.40	–	Near by area
16.	D.T.W	Phyllingkata	–	Ground Water	Direct pumping	No treatment	0.08	–	Near by village
17.	D.T.W	Betkuchi	–	Ground Water	Direct pumping	No treatment	0.15	–	Near by area
18.	D.T.W	Satgaon	–	Ground Water	Direct pumping	No treatment	0.20	–	Near by area
19.	D.T.W	Azara	–	Ground Water	Direct pumping	No treatment	0.55	–	Near by village
20.	D.T.W	Dharapur	–	Ground Water	Direct pumping	Simple treatment	0.52	–	Dharapur village

N.B. In addition, there are about 450 tube wells (ordinary suction, IM-II, IM-III) installed by GMC excluding private water sources.

1. Total installed capacity of treatment plants under GMC area = 98.0 Mld.
2. Total produciton from T.P under GMC area = 79.0 Mld
3. Total supply from D.T.W., IM-II, IM-III, T.W by GMC = 4.5 Mld
4. Total approximate present demand of water under Greater Guwahati = 165.0 Mld
5. Total water demand in 2018 under Greater Guwahati = 301.0 Mld
6. Total water demand in 2033 under Greater Guwahati = 535.5 Mld
7. Deficiency between present installed capacity and supply (98.0-79.0) (Neglecting untreated T.W. supplies) = 21.0 Mld
8. Deficiency between present demand and supply (165.0-79.0) (Neglecting untreated T.W. supplies) = 86.0 Mld

3. DEFICIENCIES OF EXISTING SYSTEM AND PROBLEMS

3.1 *The main deficiencies of the existing Water Supply Schemes are–*

- (i) Limited area/population covered.
- (ii) Water supply is intermittent for short duration and supply is not reliable.
- (iii) Distribution of water is not uniform.
- (iv) Supply pressure is low.
- (v) Leakage/wastage of water is high in the distribution system.
- (vi) Chances of pollution of water during hours of low pressure supply or no supply is high through leaky joints and valves.
- (vii) No provision is there for fire fighting.
- (viii) Laboratory facilities for water testing does not exist.
- (ix) Inadequate maintenance due to insufficient fund for maintenance activities.
- (x) Poor tariff level and inadequate revenue collection for supplying water to consumers.

3.2 *Other miscellaneous problems afflicting existing water supply system under GMC needing attention.*

(1) Intake :

- Pontoons (barge) are old, leaking heavily needs to be changed.
- Frequent choking of suction foot valves, needs improved device to avoid it.
- Irregular power supply and voltage fluctuation specially during dry season which affects water pumping.

- Problems due to long delivery hose pipe when river water level undergoes fluctuations in different seasons and specially when water level in the river recedes.

(2) Carrying capacity of old pumping main is affected. This needs attention. But this being a single main it is not disturbed now for fear of disruption of water supply.

(3) Treatment Plant (TP):

Panbazar 'GMC' water treatment plant has expired its design life. It needs renovation and augmentation with proper sludge disposal facilities. Similarly Satpukhuri TP needs renovation and augmentation.

(4) Existing laboratory facility is insignificant :

Laboratory support is a must for determining dosage of chemicals, efficiency of treatment and monitoring quality of water supplied to the consumers.

(5) Clear water pumping mains laid on hill slopes leading to clear water service reservoirs on hill tops, have severe soil erosion problems with risk of supply disruption during rainy season. This needs stabilisation.

(6) Distribution system :

- Existing distribution system is old and covers limited area. Due to road development activities, pipelines have heavy overburden of earth and many of the pipe lines are now almost in the middle of the roads and as such it has become difficult to locate and repair/replace the pipelines in many areas, in time.
- Heavy leakages exist in many pipe joints, valves, specials etc. Present leakage/wastage of water is roughly about 30-35% of production which is a costly loss for all concerned.
- Carrying capacity of ironpipe lines particularly the small dia iron pipelines have substantially reduced. This may be due to corrosion, incrustations and/or pitting of pipelines.

This need in-depth examination.

(7) • Inadequate number of trained technical operation and maintenance (O&M) staff.

• Absence of information service cell/public relation cell for attending to public complaints/grievances for quick redressal.

3.3 *Financial Problems*

(1) Inadequate fund availability for regular upkeep of various components of water supply system (*e.g.* barge, raw water main, T.P., replacement of damaged pipes/valve or stoppage of leaks in distribution pipeline etc.).

(2) Inadequate revenue collection from consumers : Monthly collection from house connections including sale proceeds from tanker supply is about Rs. 3.00 lakh (approx.) whereas, the minimum expenditure/month = Rs. 45.00 lakh.

[Salary = Rs. 14.00 lakh, Chemicals = Rs. 3.00 lakh
Energy bill = Rs. 25.00 lakh Repairs (etc.) = Rs. 3.00 lakh]

4. WHAT STEPS GMC HAS TAKEN TO IMPROVE SITUATION ?

GMC authority has formulated following project proposals and submitted the same to concerned authorities. These project proposals are :

1. A proposal amounting to Rs. 162.85 crore to cover eastern part of the city only has been submitted to HUDCO in 1999. This will benefit 6.80 lakh population. Assam Government has approved this for obtaining loan.
2. A proposal costing Rs. 115.72 crore for covering central part of the city has been submitted to UNDP through Government of Assam in 1998. It is understood that the project is under active consideration of UNDP.

3. Another project proposal of Rs. 444.61 crore to cover entire greater Guwahati area has also been submitted to UNDP through UNESCO Association Guwahati unit in 1998 by GMC.
4. A project proposal amounting Rs. 19.0 crore (approx.) has been submitted to Government of India in 1999 for obtaining Central Government assistance for improvement of existing water supply system under GMC.

Tentatively 3 new T.P. have been proposed at the following sites by G.M.C. :

(1) Ramsa Hill (Behind Holy Child School) – T.P. unit 1.

(2) Kalapahar – T.P. unit 2.

(3) Nilachal Hill– T.P. unit 3.

The Table 4.3 indicates very roughly the capacity of proposed new treatment plants (Phase-I) to meet water demand upto 2018 (in addition to existing T.P. of GMC Greater Guwahati service area). But this capacity will be drastically reduced if existing T.P. capacities are upgraded/augmented.

Table 4.3 : New water T.P. (Phase-I)

Intake Site 1	Location of T.P. 2	Capacity of T.P. (Phase-I) 3	Areas to cover 4
Kharguli	Ramsa Hill (New T.P.)	67.5 Mld	Eastern service dist. (Chandmari, Noormati, Punjabari, Beltola)
Panbazar	Kalapahar T.P. (Proposed)	88.5 Mld	Central service dist. excluding area covered by old T.P.) areas are Birubari, Barsapara, Kahilipara, Hatigaon etc.

(Contd.)

1	2	3	4
Pandughat	Nilachal (Proposed)	66.0 Mld	Western service district (part)

N.B. 1. Number and capacity of plants may undergo modification depending on the extent of augmentation possible in the existing T. Plants.

2. It is suggested that G.M.C. may study feasibility of locating 3 treatment plants at the same Ramsa Hills and design capacity of each plant for Qmax-day.

5. WHAT SHOULD BE THE FUTURE WATER SUPPLY PROJECT AREA ?

A Master Plan for water supply, sewerage and drainage was prepared in 1971 through CMPO[3] by the TCPO[4], Assam for Guwahati Metropolitan District (GMD) area. That master plan which is valid upto 2001 may need revision and TCPO should take up this work immediately, if not done already. Based on that revision and conforming to that plan only all future water supply projects are required to be taken up within greater Guwahati are to avoid chaotic condition in future.

The implementation may be taken up in phases on the basis of priority and availability of fund by any responsible agency including GMC. Initially, Greater Guwahati water supply project may cover GMC area and the adjoining fringe area situated on the south bank of Brahmaputra, North Guwahati area may be taken up at a later date considering geographical barrier and existence of present North Guwahati town water supply scheme.

6. POPULATION FORECAST AND WATER DEMAND

Population of Guwahati is increasing rapidly due to various factors, some of these are :

(a) Improved railway, river, road, and air communication

[3] CMPO – Calcutta Metopolitan Planning Organisation.

[4] TCPO – Town and Country Planning Organisation.

facilities.

(b) Availability of higher and improved educational facilities like Engineering, Medical besides Arts and Science education.

(c) City is the entrance of North East India and also it is the centre for development of commerce and industries.

(d) Guwahati is the main centre for recruitment in various states and Central services, banks, P.S.U. and is the seat of main High Court for N.E. states.

It is, therefore, necessary to consider population of greater Guwahati covering G.M.C. area and *peri*-urban area on the south bank of River Brahmaputra at a time.

On analysis of population growth as estimated by GMC in 1998 for GMC and its fringe area (on the south bank), it is observed that during 1901-91 average decade growth rate of population was 60% and that same trend is likely to continue for some more years to come. However to arrive at a realistic projected population figure, average of population figure obtained by Geometrical increase method and Incremental increase method has been adoped. Floating population has been taken as 10% of calculated population figure.

Accordingly, projected design population and water demand @150 lpcd (average) during design period has tentatively been shown in Table-4.4.

Table 4.4 : Design Population and Water Demand

Year	Population in GMC area	Pupulation outside GMC area	Total	Water require-ment (Mld)	Including 10%floating population (Mld)
2001	802,229	192,840	995,069	149.26	164.19
2018 (Phase-I)	1,469,260	353,181	1,822,441	273.37	300.70
2033 (Phase-II)	2,615,579	628,735	3,244,314	486.65	535.31

7. CHOICE OF RAW WATER SOURCE : WHY RIVER SOURCE & NOT GROUND WATER CHOSEN?

7.1 *Ground Water*

In Guwahati, ground water is confined to some limited isolated pockets only. Even if ground water meets present demand and is apparently a least cost solution, it is not recommended because of following reasons:

(1) Availability of ground water is limited to some pockets.

(2) Unsatisfactory performance of tube wells.

(3) Presence of higher percentage of minerals and some of these are beyond permissible limit needing treatment of ground water.

(4) Life of tube well is short to be economical in the long run. It is about 10 years.

(5) Economical integration/collection of different wells yield to a central treatment plant is not feasible in case of large city. For this a number of raw water pumping main will have to be laid which is uneconomical.

(6) Gradual reduction in open surface area required for recharging of underground aquifer leading to gradual decline of well/yield with age of well.

7.2 *Surface Source*

Nearby River Brahmaputra is a reliable surface source.

7.2.1 ***Quantity : As per available record —***

Average discharge of Brahmaputra is4500m^3/s

Highest W.L. recorded on 29-9-88	45.40m
Lowest W.L. recorded on 28-1-86	40.80m

7.2.2 *Quality*

Raw water quality of the river water is indicated in the Table 4.1B and 4.1C. It is observed that raw water quality at intake sites is more deteriorated in the downstream side of the city starting from Kharguli to Saraighat.

This trend is mainly due to discharge of untreated domestic waste water from urban community into Brahmaputra river. Ideal situation would have been to locate raw water intakes at the upstream of the city avoiding as far as possible these waste water outfalls.

8. WATER SUPPLY FOR GREATER GUWAHATI : — SOME OBSERVATIONS

8.1 *Water Treatment Plant*

Basing on analysis report, conventional treatment plant can be adopted for treating raw river water. But for high bacteriological contamination, adoption of improved disinfection method is necessary in place of existing practice of using bleaching powder solution. To take care of THM, pesticides etc., appropriate treatment process may be adopted.

As raw water turbidity load of the river water is likely to shoot upto 2000 NTU or more on rainy days at times, extra care is necessary to reduce turbidity load before putting raw water into conventional treatment plant in order to

(a) reduce problems in operation of valves, its wear and tear and thus increasing life of valves.

(b) reduce requirement of chemical doses and thereby effect economy.

It is suggested that a plain sedimentation basin of 10-15 min detention time with 10-25 m/h surface loading may be provided ahead of main T.P.

Location of T.P. should take into consideration the following aspects :

(a) Availability of T.P. site with sludge disposal facility and scope for future expansion.

(b) Proximity of treatment plant to the intake point.

(c) Proximity of treatment plant to reliable power source.

(d) Availability of stable/erosion free intake site with easy approach.

(e) Absence of immediate upstream pollution.

(f) Avoiding long raw water pumping man.

8.2 *Old Water Treatment Plant*

The old GMC water treatment plant at Panbazar has expired its design life but still it can effectively serve the central district under GMC area if it is augmented.

This augmentation/upgradation can be done without much change of existing structures by introducing improved technologies like use of tube settlers, dual or multimedia filters, improving sludge disposal facilities and efficiency of chemical coagulation in the plant by using polyelectrolytes. However, all these will need in-depth study of existing structures of all existing units and parameters, structural configuration, dimension of old hydro-clarifiers, hydraulic flow sheets etc.

Similarly the 2.5 mgd (11.25 mld) T.P. of PHED and 5 mgd (22.5 mld) plant of Satpukhuri can also be upgraded without much structural change.

It should be kept in mind that plants should preferably be centralised or few in number in order to effect economy and having better management.

8.3 *Water Distribution*

Considering (1) geographical and topographical barrier, (2) contiguity of populated area, (3) Convenience of water supply and ease of O&M and (4) overall economy, Greater Guwahati water supply project area may be divided into three main service districts with different zones under this for distributions as follows :

(a) Eastern service district
(b) Western service district
(c) Central service district.

In the design of distribution system within the service districts, provision for fire fighting facilities and required water reserve as per as code of practice should be kept in consultation with local fire service authority specially for high value riskprone districts/zones.

24 hours water supply under adequate pressure is more ideal than intermittent supply but number of maintenance staff may be high raising cost of O & M higher. Pipelines designed for 24 hours supply will be smaller in size and thereby economise capital cost. Both aspects may be considered at the detail design stage of the projects.

If water supply is metered, additional facility/infrastructure for metre-repairing locally should be thought of in advance at the project preparation stage. Without these facility and infrastructure, adoption of meter system will not work satisfactorily.

In peri-urban areas, where adoption of sewerage system is necessary, water distribution pipelines can be designed for 125 lpcd and where there is no chance of adoption of sewerage, the water distribution pipelines can be designed for 70-100 lpcd as per suggestion of Government of India working group. It is to be pointed out here that, in high demand districts of GMC, the actual consumption of water is higher than 150 lpcd because of many nursing homes etc. but at the same time consumption in the fringe area will be lower. Hence the average 150 lpcd is recommended.

The capacity of zonal service reservoirs should be properly assessed keeping in mind the water demand pattern of the zones and need for fire reserve etc.

9. RECOMMENDATIONS

A. Immediate Short Term Measures

(1) Capacity of existing treatment plants be increased to its installed capacity by renovating the plant. Along with this, improvement of raw water instake and replacement/repair of raw water pumpsets and distribution pipe system be done. Feasibility of upgradation/augmentation of treatment plant (T.P.) capacity by adopting modern technologies also be examined.

(2) A new service reservoir adjacent to or above the existing 61 mld (13.5 gallons) capacity reservoir be constructed so that distribution of water can be done under adequate pressure to the present low pressure zone with necessary flow adjustment.

(3) As an immediate measure to improve water supply situation

- All leakages which are evident or reported must be rectified within a time frame of 1-2 months by Guwahati Municipal Corporation (GMC), Public Health Engineering Department (PHED) and Assam Urban's Water Supply and Sewerage Board (AUWS & SB) in their respective jurisdiction.
- Direct pumping of water from pumping main be stopped. Existing public taps, reportedly more than 400 in number, are a major source of wastage of water for having no form of definite ownership responsibility. These should either be relocated with group ownership responsibility and charged for water in order to reduce the wastage or alternative measures be taken to contain this wastage/ misuse.

  Supply of water is a service and every service has to be paid for as this will create a sense of ownership and responsibility among consumers. If desired supply to this section of people may be cross-subsidised.

(4) Chlorine gas or liquid chlorine be used for disinfection of (drinking) water in place of existing practice of using

bleaching powder solution. Similarly, the coagulation system is inadequate. This should be improved.

B. *Long Term Measures*

(1) The Master Plan for Water Supply, Sewerage and Drainage for GMD prepared by CMPO (valid upto 2001) or as revised/updated should be followed in preparation of new water supply project for Greater Guwahati by GMC or any other agency.
While deciding capacities of new plants, augmented capacity of existing plant be taken into consideration.
Implementation may be done in phases as per fund position by different competent agencies.

(2) Only one authority should be empowered to examine all water supply and drainage schemes which should invariably conform to the requirements as specified in the Master Plan.

(3) Actual updated number of house connections under GMC should be maintained. Wardwise physical survey be conducted soon within GMC area to ascertain number of legal connections and illegal *tappings made*.

(4) Present water tariff collection system is required to be reviewed and improved. Tariff should be raised to meet the water supply operation and maintenance (O & M) charges atleast. It is applicable to all agencies including PHED.
Water supply wing under GMC be given authority and power to collect water charges separately and allowed to maintain and operate this through a separate account for the purpose of O & M. For this, necessary staff, infrastructure for billing, collection of charges etc. be provided.

(5) For giving any new house connection, house owners must make covered tanks in their premises at their own cost and GMC will lay a pipeline ending in the same tank with a float valve inside the tank. No tap connection from this

line be allowed. Cost of laying this line including float valve be realised in one instalment as agreement to give this connection. For this purpose, before sanctioning any new building plan within city area it may be ensured by GMC that provision of water tank is included in the building plan.

(6) A properly equipped centralised water testing laboratory having facilities for complete physical, chemical and bacteriological examination of water be established and each individual plant be provided its own mini lab to determine turbidily, pH and chemical doses daily.

(7) Water at the present intake sites are bacteriologicaly contaminated. New intake site as far as practicable should be located upstream of city proper and treatment plants be centralised to the extent feasible and constructed near raw water intakes.

(8) Distribution system should be properly designed with adequate terminal pressure and provision kept for fire-fighting/ fire hydrants at important road crossings/ points in consultation with local fire service authority.

(9) Pumping of silt and sand laden raw water through long pumping main be avoided as far as practicable.

(10) Technical personnel involved in water supply be trained to assess and solve practical problems encountered. The existing water supply wing of GMC which is being called upon to play vital role in this utility service, be restructured. A field division headed by an Executive Engineer with two field sub-divisions service areawise be created. A technical branch with AEE/AE is also essential. CE may be in charge of overall supervision, planning, administration and coordination.

(11) Adequate fund for essential O & M activities be provided on priority basis.

(12) A centralised public relation/information cell with telephone facility is to be established and manned by a suitable person to attend to public grievances for quick redressal. At present, there is no communication facilities between different intakes, treatment plants, booster stations/

reservoirs and controlling centre which is necessary for better co-ordination in operation, control and supply.

(13) One centralised storage facility to store urgently required material like valves, tools, pipes, pumps etc. for emergency work is essential.

10. CONCLUSION

Water is basic necessity of life. But present water supply situation in Guwahati by and large is alarming and is worsening rapidly.

It is, therefore, essential that a comprehensive water supply project for entire Greater Guwahati area may be planned and implemented with due consideration to the existing Master Plan requirements and existing water T.P. facilities available including those of NFR and IOC. Any more delay may complicate the situation further beyond control and even cause law and order problem.

In brief, the present water problem in Guwahati is essentially that of supply and management (both financial and maintenance) and not of availability.

ACKNOWLEDGEMENT

The authors wish to thank Dr. K. L. Chakravarty, Public Analyst, Govt. of Assam for providing data for Tables- 4.1A and 4.1B. Thanks are also due to Shri H Sarkar, M.D. and Shri A. Deka A.E., AUWS & SB, Guwahati, Shri Sujit Kalita A.E., Water Wing, GMC and Shri B. Baishya, Addl.C.E. PHED for rendering assistance in preparation of paper.

REFERENCES

Culcutta Mertopolitan Planning Organisation, 1971, Master Plan for Water Supply Sewerage and Drainage for Guwahati Metropolitan District—1971—2001(prepared for TCPO, Govt. of Assam).

Setup Consultant, Calcutta, 1990 DPR for Water Supply Scheme, Greater Guwahati city, 1990 (prepared for AUWS&SB).

The Hindu, Survey of the environment, 1994.

GMC, 1998, DPR Proposal for Water Supply Scheme of Greater Guwahati Under UNESCO/UNDP.

ANNEXURE-I

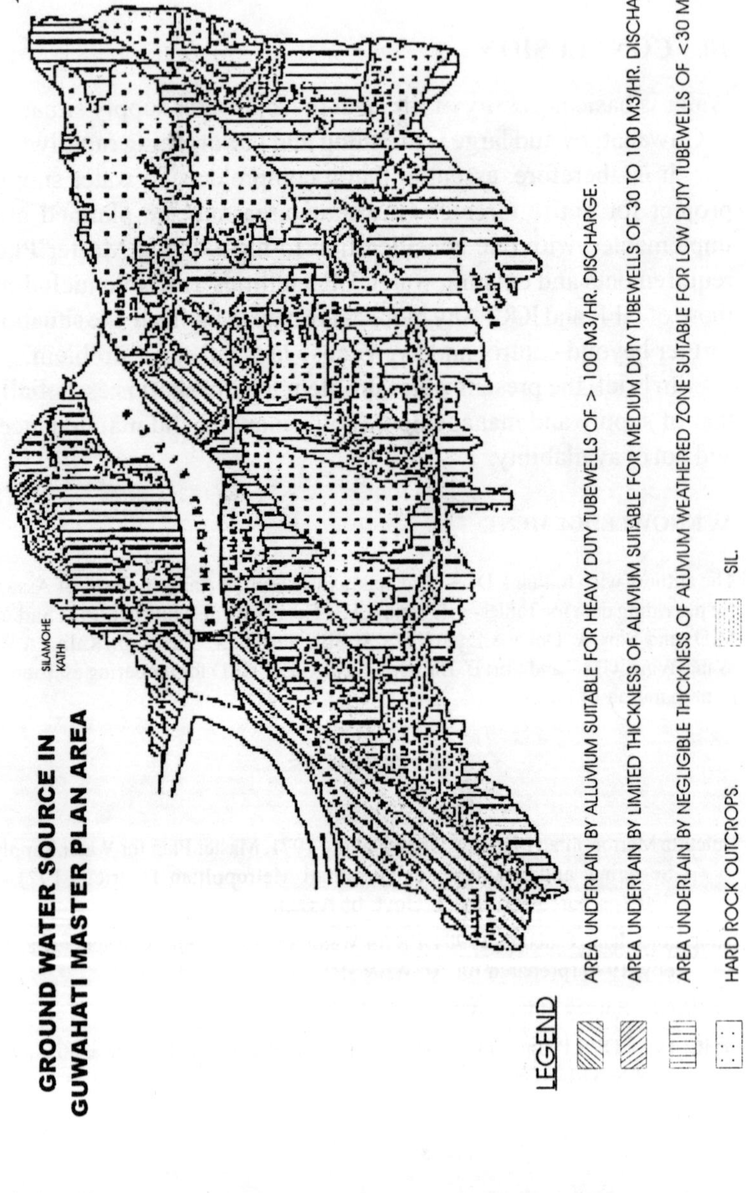
GROUND WATER SOURCE IN
GUWAHATI MASTER PLAN AREA
SILAMOHE
KATHI
LEGEND
AREA UNDERLAIN BY ALLUVIUM SUITABLE FOR HEAVY DUTY TUBEWELLS OF > 100 M3/HR. DISCHARGE.
AREA UNDERLAIN BY LIMITED THICKNESS OF ALLUVIUM SUITABLE FOR MEDIUM DUTY TUBEWELLS OF 30 TO 100 M3/HR. DISCHARGE.
AREA UNDERLAIN BY NEGLIGIBLE THICKNESS OF ALUVIUM WEATHERED ZONE SUITABLE FOR LOW DUTY TUBEWELLS OF <30 M3/HR. DISCHARGE.
HARD ROCK OUTCROPS.
SIL.

5

PROBLEMS OF POTABLE WATER IN GUWAHATI CITY

Kamlesh Kalita & Aswini Kr. Borah

Introduction

Water is one of the most complex natural resources that demands a very comprehensive understanding of its inherent features in occurrence and distribution for an integrated planning aimed at an optimum development for agriculture, health, industry, power and transport sectors of a country. Demand for water is constantly increasing in the various countries of the world with the increase of population, to provide better living conditions to human habitations, more irrigation facilities for raising agricultural produce in the field of agriculture, for different industrial sectors and also for nuclear and space programmes (Chorelay, 1969). Needless to say that water has been and in future it will always be an important resource for sustenance of the human being in the world. However, of late the world community is facing water crisis and as such it now calls for urgent steps to be taken to preserve and judicious use of the same. Presently more than 1.2 billion people in the developing countries of the world are lacking the access of safe drinking water apart from its other uses. The scenario in India which is also a developing country regarding potable water is not better. Always there is a gap between the demand and supply of the potable water in major cities of India, though civic bodies like Municipal Corporation or government bodies like Public Health Engineering Department etc. are there to provide potable waters to the residents of the cities. Potable water is one which is necessarily safe and good to drink that is colourless, odourless and pleasant in taste (Sharma and Sharma, 1996) and it is the duty of the civic bodies to provide the same to the residents of cities/towns and to resident of other areas. Unfortunately, this potable aspect of water many times is ignored (Laskar, 1999) and that gives rise to problems relating to human health hazards.

Statement of the Problem

Coming to N.E. India we find that among all the cities of the region Guwahati is considered as the premier city and very often it is called as the gateway city of N. E. India. Now, over last three decades due to increase of population in this city the problem of potable water is increasing and presently a vast gap between the demand and supply of the same is noticed. Hence, in this paper an attempt is made to discuss the problems of potable water in Guwahati city.

Objective of the Study

1. To study the prevailing scenario of potable and related problems.
2. To suggest some measures for providing potable water.

Methodology

To fulfil the various needs of the study, the authors collected the data from various government and private agencies and also used observation method. Further, interview technique was also used to get the required data from the cross-section of the residents of Guwahati city.

Field of Study

For the present study Guwahati city is taken as the field of study. The city of Guwahati is an undulating plain which is located on the foothills of Meghalaya Plateau. The city area as defined by the Guwahati Municipal Corporation is from Bondajan river in the east to Khanajan river in the west. It is extended from the mighty river Brahmaputra in the north to National Highway No. 37 and Garbhanga reserve forest in the south. The total area of the city is about 300 sq. kms. The present population is about 6 lakh within the corporation area of the city.

Discussion and Findings

From the present study it is observed that about 70% area of this ever expanding city is not having any proper provision for potable water. Only 30% area is only covered by the existing Guwahati Municipal Corporation, Public Health Engineering Department of the Government of Assam and Assam Urban Development Board.

The study revealed that the present requirement of potable water in the city is 150 million litres per day whereas only 55 million litres of the same is being supplied everyday the authorities mentioned in the immediate anterior paragraph. The irony of the fact that for remaining 95 million litres the residents of the city are facing number of problems everyday and they have no other alternative but to depend on private sources like tubewells, wells, deep tubewells and the Brahmaputra river— in which potable question raises serious doubts.

Leakage of water from the water pipes of Guwahati city is a regular phenomenon. The flooding of streets of Guwahati city at different areas are caused through bursting of pipes and breaking of pipe joints. It is observed from the study that the pipes laid down in many places are of PVC material and of asbestos which are unable to withstand the high pressure of water from inside and also of outside jerks caused by heavy vehicles mainly at the road crossings etc. (PHED, Govt. of Assam, 1999, Barman, 1998). Our study reveals that in some places of Guwahati city *viz*., R. G. Baruah Road, A. T. Road near overbridge the leakage of supply water is about 32% and which is very alarming.

In Guwahati city over exploitation of ground water through modern means of well installation and pumping arrangement is the root cause of going down of ground water level in various areas (DGM, Govt. of Assam, 1999). According to a report of Central Ground Water Board the ground water level in many parts of Guwahati city has been falling since 1977. In the year 1977 the ground water could be strucked at an average depth of 6 metres, whereas the deepest ground water level was recorded to be around of 16 metres below the land surface. In the year 1983 the ground water level reached an average depth of 25 metres. Further, it has been recorded that the drop of ground water level by 4 to 5 metres in a span of only 12 years, i.e. from 1983 to 1995. Alarmingly there are certain areas in the city where the falling of ground water level is increasingly being noticed. Mention may be made in this connection about the area like Basistha basin which covers the areas around Hatigaon-Dispur, Lachit Nagar-Ulubari and Gota Nagar etc. Now due to the falling of the ground water level the salinity and brackish problem are gradually on the increase in some parts of the city like Srimantapur etc.

Presently to tide over the problem of potable water in Guwahati city two ambitious projects are being undertaken with the fund available from HUDCO (Rs. 162 crores) and UNESCO (Rs. 62 crores) and the target date of the completion of the projects are on 2018. It is hoped that with the completion of these two projects potable water problem in Guwahati city would be solved considerably in future provided the population growth in the city is kept to the optimum level and with the development of satellite towns away from it. But leaving the future scenario the need of the hour is to take some active steps to solve the present problems of potable water in Guwahati city hence the present authors are giving some suggestions in the suggestion part of the present paper.

Suggestions

1. The whole equipments of providing drinking water to the residents of the city should be phased out systematically and the same may be replaced by new sophisticated equipments.
2. The city of Guwahati and its surrounding areas receive abundant rainfall and this rainfall is responsible for causing inundation of

low lying areas of the city during the rainy season. Arrangement may be made to store such water for domestine use through proper harvesting which would solved the drainage problem and also the problem of drinking water to a considerable extent.

3. The Government of Assam should have some control over imposition of Ground Water Regulation Act of 1997 as ground water is a state subject.
4. Exploratory and production well drilling of ground water should be made as per the Hydrological Potential Map prepared by the Directorate of Geology and Mining of the Government of Assam.
5. The garbage of the city should be managed properly so that it does not pollute the ground and surface water in the city.
6. Evaluation and regular monitoring of the water supply system of the city would help the system itself more effective and efficient.

Conclusion

To conclude it is hoped that in order to have the effective approach in potable water management of the city the concerning authority should supervise, execute and maintain the whole system in a well coordinated manner.

Acknowledgement

The authors of this paper are indebted to Prof. N.N. Bhattacharyya, Deptt. of Geography, Gauhati University for his valuable guidance in writing the paper.

References

Barman, D.K. (1998, March, 29), 'Urban Water Problem in Guwahati City', *The Assam Tribune*, Guwahati.

Choreley, R.J. (ed.) (1969), *Water, Earth and Man*, London, Methuen.

Directorate of Geology and Mining, Government of Assam, Guwahati, Personal

Interview with the Officials of the Directorate by Mr. Kamalesh Kalita, one of the co-authors of the paper.

Laskar, M.A. (1999,12 August), 'Water Security for India in the 21st Century', *The Assam Tribune*, Guwahati.

Public Health Engineering Department, Government of Assam, Guwahati, Personal Interview with the Officials of the Department by Mr. Kamalesh Kalita, one of the co-authors of the paper.

Sharma, R.K. and Sharma, T.K. (1969), *A Text Book of Hydrology and Water Resources Engineering*, New Delhi, Dhanpat Rai & Sons.

6

DEVELOPMENT PROBLEMS OF THE GUWAHATI

Kabindra Hazarika

The city of Guwahati covers an area of about 262.00 square kilometre under the master plan area out of which 215.00 square kilometres is under Municipal Corporation area. At present city spreads about 10.00 km. in the North-South direction and about 27.00 km in the East-West direction.

The population of Guwahati as per census of the year 1971 was about 1,24,000 and rose to about 6,00,000 as per 1991 census, indicating growth of population to be more than 380% during the decade. It can, therefore, be assumed that since 1991 upto the present time city population even at this growth rate rose to about 8,00,000. This rapid increase of population of the city coupled with its importance in terms of being centre of social, commercial, educational, political and industrial activities made the city to be most important centre of entire North-Eastern region of the Country. These has resulted rapid expansion of the urban areas at a very fast pace almost beyond the control of authorities entrusted with planning and development actions and regulation of the city works. The growth of industry in the last decade in and around Guwahati has been phenomenal and things have been moving so fast, that there has been no time to think out the best methods of arranging for the new type of life and habitation which industrialism has bought into being. Facilities for earning one's livelihood lure people to the city from their congested but economically under-developed villages and causing overcrowding of already congested areas. The Guwahati City is growing in volume on the east-west direction by converting neighbouring villages into suburban which in course of time also become badly congested due to unplanned growth. In the absence of strict enforcement of provision of bye-laws by competent authorities, location of industry in residential areas, shops in areas which are more suitable for other purposes, educational institution in environments not suitable to students is a common sight and this sort of displacement grows together with the diversity of population.

All the residents and visitors to Guwahati are now facing the problems in terms of reduction of basic civic amenities. The different problems faced in this city such as growth of buildings, drinking water, drainage and waterlogging, rain flood, sewerage and sanitation. Traffic and transportation, roads, educational facilities and amusement and other social amenities, needs to be tackled by joint efforts of the citizens and Government authorities.

Growth of Building

The present trend of building construction in Guwahati is now mostly apartment type buildings of high-rise structures. This trend is basically due to scarcity of habitable land and preference for central location with people wishing to live in close proximity to the centres of employment and business along with security reason. Though modern technology has made possible the design and construction of high rise buildings to any limit on vertical expansion, except those imposed by civic authorities and financial consideration, such haphazard construction may create parleying situation to city life for non-availability of adequate civic amenities to the increased population. Since same road network will have to be used, they are bound to be overcrowded. This aspect of the problem is very much relevant to Guwahati where most of the densly populated localities are served by narrow roads which are inadequate even for present population. The rapid growth of vertical expansion of the buildings in Guwahati is not suitable in areas where percentage of roads and streets is a small percentage of total land area, from the environmental consideration as well as the capacity to cope with increase traffic and drainage volume. Since Guwahati is situated in the most seismical sensitive zone in India with record of frequent and sever earthquakes, and not condition for support of heavy foundations of high rise buildings is too poor, construction of such building requires careful design and supervision of construction works by competent structural engineer, which should be made obligatory on the part of builders or owners of such buildings. To ensure safety of construction of such structures without any future hazard to occupants and adjacent structures, builders, owners, planners, designers are to be made fully responsible and accountable in all respect for any danger from construction and design defects.

Since with the growth of high rise buildings in Guwahati, number of problems cropped up in a locality even though there are statutory regulations by civic authorities for such construction in the city. It is felt that infringement of bye-law provisions are taking place frequently and to avert such situation strict check of construction works as per permission granted by the authority should be made by them at fixative intervals and proper action taken as per rule in time, for all unauthorised construction

For construction of buildings in the city, following points appears to be pertinent to be mentioned for consideration of concerned authorities :

(1) Finished ground level of the plot of land should be fixed by the civic authorities granting permission for construction at the locality, instead of practice of arbitrary fixation of G.L. and link level by owner/builder.

(2) Location where existing traffic and drainage facilities are not adequate, construction of high rise buildings should be allowed only with reduced height of the building than that of bye-law provision.

(3) A suitable regulation for height/width ratio should be included the bye-laws for safety against overturning due to earthen and stability of the building.

(4) There should be strict quality control on the construction of high rise buildings.

(5) Fire fighting

Water Supply

Existing water supply facilities of the city by P.H.E.D., Municipality, Urban water supply and Sevage Board hardly cater to the need to 25% of present population of the city. With the rapid increase in construction of high rise buildings in the city, deep tube wells are installed by owners for water supply to their premises, as a result of which adjacent residents having ring wells, hand pump, tube wells etc., as water supply sources are facing serve water scarcity for lowering of ground water levels. As such for installation of deep tube wells for buildings, strict restriction should be imposed by concerned authority with special regulation making it binding on the part of the owner/builder to obtain flexibility report from Ground Water Board or similar Government agency about sufficiency of the water bearing strata to meet the demand without causing inconvenience to other residents of the locality.

The unchecked installation of deep tube wells may lower ground water levels of the city in some localities to an extent which can cause extensive settlement of the ground level and may endanger existing structures.

The river Brahmaputra is flowing by the side of the city and, therefore, it is felt quite possible to supply adequate potable water to the entire population of the city by taking up comprehensive water supply project keeping in view the immediate and future requirement of the growing city. Finance for such project may be raised by issue of long term Government security bond giving annual return with bonus. Expenditure that may be incurred in completing the project as well as in operation and maintenance of the plants can be meet up from revenue collection from sale of water to consumers.

In the hilly areas of the city survey can be conducted for the possibility of collecting rain water during rainy season, by constructing large tanks on the top of the hills as well as at valley found suitable for the purpose. Water collected at tanks may help residents of the locality in meeting their water demand in lean season and shall reduce the runoff from the hills during rainy season and check soil erosion.

Traffic, Transportation, Roads

Guwahati is the foremost city in the entire North East region having direct rail, road and air links with rest of the country. The inland water service through regular steamer from Guwahati to Calcutta as existed before partition is also appears to be at the verge of collapsing.

For the strategic location, the city generates large volume of percentage and goods traffic to and from the city mainly by road and rail. Guwahati is the focal point of distribution of goods for Meghalaya state in addition to other district of the state. In Guwahati road network system was not planned properly in past which has now posed considerable problems in the efficient movement of traffic. Though about 10% of land is allocated to transport and communication of as per land use on Guwahati Master Plan there is hardly any relationship before road network system and landuse activities. All most important damages experience considerable set back due to poor road geometrical mainly at the road intersection areas.

The growth of traffic volume in major arterial roads of the city has been phenomenal during the last few years. Fast moving vehicles registered an annual growth of around 10 per cent. It is clearly evident from the fact that the manner in which the growth of vehicles make their impact on the existing road system, the transport system in city roads specially at G.N.B. Road, A.T. Road virtually come to threshold limit of traffic operation to taste the prevailing situation for efficiently traffic flow and safety of road... detail traffic and transportation plan should be prepared by concerned authorities and priorities identified for implementation through existing authorities.

In connection with traffic problems of the city, following points are suggested and brought to notice for consideration of concerned authorities if found viable.

(1) Survey should be conducted jointly with Railway authority to find out the possibility of construction of road-cum-drains of width 5.00 metres on the both sides of railway line which is now running through the heart of the city in east-west direction. This road-cum-drain should be able to carry only light vehicles, cycle-rickshaws, thelas and other animal driven carts.

(2) For cause of traffic congestion of G.N.B.Road specially for the stretch between T.C. School and Chandmari during morning peak hours from 8.30 A.M. to 11.30 and evening peak hours from 4.00 P.M. to 6.00 P.M. One way traffic flow operation excluding city buses and cycle rikshaws may be tried diverting the plying of other light vehicles through other new roads such as Pubsarania-Gandhibasti-Islampur Road, Nizarapar-Silpukhuri-Chenikuthi Road, after improving these roads including geometrical improvement of existing vertical curves.

(3) To ensure that road safety is achieved to the possible extent, provision of Zebra crossing at road intersections, pedestrian signal, improvement of geometric of the road junction, road accident warning sign boards etc. are necessary.

(4) The road along railway line to T.C. School can be improved as a link road with one way traffic circulation to relieve the congestion on G.N.B. Road.

(5) To reduce the number of city bus stops upto the optimum level and to regulate the stoppages for different route buses on the common stretch only at alternate stops. Passenger movement study should be conducted first for each of the existing bus stops of select stops for city buses of different routes.

(6) Authorise bus stands at Chandmari, University colony, which

are now existing on the main road itself should be shifted to available spaces of nearby link roads. Car parking area around Silpukhuri tank should be improved to provide better parking facility. Parking of vehicles on road sides except at selected places should be strictly dealt as per rule by conceived authentic as a deterrent to the prevailing practice. Carriage way of roads should not be allowed to be used as a garrage for the vehicle at night, which is a common sight at present.

Drainage

The problem of drainage in Guwahati is becoming very acute day by day. The drainage facilities available for the city are the river Bharalu, Basistha river, Silsako Bil, Chola Bil, Dipar Bil and also low marshy areas, which act, as impounding reservoirs during rainy season. All these bills and rivers releases the drainge water into the river Brahmaputra.

With the exception of developed areas like refinery, railway and cantonment, there is no planned and efficient drainage network for the city. With increase in population density, spurt is building construction activities, resulted filling of the bills, low marshy areas. Encroachment along the side of existing drainage channels reduced the hydraulic capacity of the drains and even with a moderate shower of short duration some of the city areas become flooded with highly polluted sewage start from May to October of the year. Highest single day rainfall is about 126 mm and the highest total rainfall of a month is about 520 mm. An average single day rainfall is enough to impound the Bharalu River full upto the bank provided the disposal of drainage water is not gone through the sluice gate at Bharalumukh during rainy days. The coverage ran off co-efficient of the drainage area is about 0.90 to 0.70 depending upon the development of the area.

The existing basins of the Guwahati performing the natural drainage of its area are as follows :

(a) *Bharalu Basin :* This basin is situated centrally has its east the Silsako bil, Meghalaya hill on South, Dipar basin at west and hill ranges from Kharguli hills, Nabagrah hills and Chunsali hill near Guwahati Refinery. River Bharalu drains Municipal area with outflow into Brahmaputra at Bharalumukh.

(b) *Silsako Basin :* This basin is at east of Guwahati and connected with Brahmaputra river though Bondazan.

(c) *Dipar Basin :* This basin is situated on South and the river Basistha from Meghalaya discharges into this basin. Through river Khanajan the basin is joined with Brahmaputra.

The natural drainage becomes ineffective during rainy season as water level of the Brahmaputra rises. During the period sluice gates remain closed to prevent back flow through drainage channels and basins become flooded due to surface runoff collected by the drainage channels.

For disposal of the impounded water of the city, pumping out water at Bharalumukh from the river Bharalu during high flood period is made and to some extent water level of the river is reduced to possible limit.

The Mora Bharalu river which joins the Bharalu river near Fatasil, during flood period flows towards south and outfalls into river Basistha and jointly flow to Dipar Bil after crossing N.H. R.C.C. bridge at Kahabari. The State Flood Control Department had proposed to link Dipar Bil with the river Kulsi with a linking channel to reduce H.F.L. of Dipar Bil to create the required water level difference for carrying discharge from the Bharalu river through Mora Bharalu river to the Dipar Bil which may reduce impounded water level to the city during the rainy days. For proper flow of water through Mora Bharalu from the river Bharalu when sluice gates are closed for rise in water level of river Brahmaputra, it has to be kept in proper condition by removing all obstructions and encroachment made on the channel including regarding and resections as per design.

The Silsoko Bil on the eastern side of the city is linked with river Brahmaputra through Bondajan. The backflow from Brahmaputra through the channel during flood period has been stopped by construction of sluice gates and been on Bondajan. This Bill should be maintained and developed by dredging to enable it to absorb sudden storm discharges. All encroachments made on the Bil area should be removed and preserve its impounding capacity for rain flood intact.

Earth filling of the bil area for construction activities should not be allowed by authorities in any case. Reduction on the impounding capacity of this bill in particular by any means shall immediately submerge the higher land around the bil area upto R.G. Baruah Road and G.S. Road aggravating the water logging problem of the city.

Within the Guwahati Municipal area, the G.N.B. Road along with adjoining areas in the south down to river Bharalu are most flood affected area due to storm run off from adjacent hills when there is a moderately heavy shower during rainy days. Inadequate soil stabilisation of the adjacent hills degraded due to indiscriminate hill cutting causes flow of huge quantity of hill sand and soil particles along the slopes to the drains which becomes chocked and incapable to drain storm water, properly resulting flooding of the area including G.N.B. Road with highly polluted sewage water. To prevent such occurrence, retardation of the degraded hills with terrace cutting, planting vegetable, quick growing creepers, shrubs etc. should be made to absorb surface runoff by the hill side. Provision of waste water drains constructed in series along the hill slope with moderate grade at higher level than H.F.L. of the rain Brahmaputra with several outlets to discharge into the river may also lessens the present storm runoff from the high area which is now flowing like torrential hilly streams. At the foothill of the hill ranges on the northern side of G.N.B. Road construction of silt traps along with a connecting drain may also reduce to silt volume now carried by linking drains from the foothill to G.N.B. Road Ride drains. There should be more railway culvěrts on the railway line on the stretch from Bamunimaidan upto railway station for quick discharge of storm runoff, which is now flooding G.N.B. road in many areas for want of adequate outlet.

It is a common sight in Guwahati to find almost all the road side drains filled with either highly polluted stagnant water or filled with growth of weeds, bushes, obstructions etc. during the lean period, from which one has to inform about defective design of drains mainly to geometric shape, bed slope, which perhaps need immediate attention of the constructing agency for necessary modification so that road side drain can act for storm water runoff as well as for small runoff of the lean period efficiently. Preparation of a detail contour map of the Guwahati showing contour intervals of 0.5 metre by the development departments of the state with the aid of Survey of India, may be very helpful in preparing drainage planning as well as other construction activities.

Sewerage

The citizens of the Guwahati City should be provided with the benefit of modern sewerage system, instead of conventional septic tanks, for preventing discharge of septic tank effluents to drains, as in many parts of the city water supply pipelines are paning through drains.

Electricity

Master Plan for electrical system in conformity with landuse plan as per Master Plan of the Guwahati should be passed by concerned authority and supplied to all development departments, agency, city lighting should be centrally monitored to minimize operational deficiencies.

Telephone

P & T Department in collaboration with P.W.D. (Roads) should evolve means for laying underground telephone cables in a manner to prevent current practice of digging the roads frequently .

Lastly it is anticipated that all concerned citizens of the Guwahati and development agencies with co-operation among themselves can solve the problems as early as possible.

7

WATER LOGGING INUNDATION PROBLEMS OF GREATER GUWAHATI
A Geographical Study

S. Sharma

Introduction

(a) *Study Area*

Guwahati is the premier urban centre of Northeast Region of India known as the 'Gateway of north-east'. It lies at the point of intersection of 26° 10'45" north latitude and 90° 45'00" east longitude. The total area of Greater Guwahati is 243.2 sq. km. including a small area of 23 sq. km. in the north of the river Brahmaputra, known by the name North Guwahati.

(b) *Drainage*

The master drain Brahmaputra river has been aligned longitudinally and it flows east to west direction segmenting Greater Guwahati into North Guwahati in the north and the core city in the south.

On the north bank of the river Brahmaputra the river Ghorajan and Barnadi maintaining their natural courses and discharge into Brahmaputra. These two rivers are not harmful to the dwellers of the North Guwahati.

On the south bank of river Brahmaputra there are as many as five tributaries such as Bharalu, Mora Bharalu, Barapani, Khanajan and Bondaijan. Bharalu is the most harmful tributary to the city dwellers, which flows through the alluvial depression of Guwahati Municipal Corporation area to meet at Bharalumukh. Bondajan in the east and Khanajan in the west both rivers originate from Silsako Beel and Dipar Beel respectively. Backflow of water from the river Brahmaputra through Bharalu, Khanajan and Bondajan cause floods frequently in every summer.

(c) *Relief*

The original city is located within a crescent shaped basin, surrounded by a number of hillocks. The hills are outliers of the Meghalaya Plateau, predominantly residual in character. They are composed of granites and gneissic rocks with the outer surface fairly weathered and contain red soil. The hills have steep slope but from the base, the slopes become gradual up to the riverbank of the north. As a result, an undulating topography has emerged with swamps and low-lying areas in between. The original settlements were mostly located on the elevated plains and the foot hill zone. Thus, the low-lying areas, smooth terrain and some hillocks of different elevations present a peculiar relief to the area.

The benchmark of the G.T.S. (Great Trigonometrical Survey) near Deputy Commissioner Office is 54.75 m. While 52.20m is recorded near Railway Station above M.S.L. with an average elevation of 51.3m for the southern bank of Brahmaputra and it rises up towards Kharghuli and Chittrachal (Navagraha) hill in the east (216 m) and Nilachal hill (303 m) in the central part. The average elevation of the low-lying areas is 49m and the lowest is 41.16m above the M.S.L. This land gradually rises to Khasi and Jaintia hills to a maximum elevation of 575m, which ends in the southern boundary of Guwahati. Again, there are areas near Chittrachal hills with a general elevation 182m towards the east and to the southern plains of 49m elevation. In between the Khasi hills and the

Brahmaputra river lies the Sarania hills (250 m), the Fastasil hill range (358 m) and the Kalapahar Narakasur hills (200-300 m). A vast low-lying area of Dipar Beel occupies more than 54 sq. km. on the western part of the city.[1] Moreover, there are low-lying plains intervened by scattered swamps and marshes in between the hills, extending from east to west. These low-lying areas are inundated often at the time of heavy rainfall.

Data Base and Methodology

For geographical location of study area, Survey of India topographical sheet No. 78 N/12 and 78 N/16, of R.F. 1: 63360 (scale 1 inch to a mile) are used and prepared a map of Greater Guwahati. It depicts various features of topography, characteristics of rivers, tributaries, settlement pattern and transport network etc. To find out the average slope of the area, the C.K. Wentworth formula has been applied on a contour map of above mentioned sheets. The formula is given below:

$$\tan\theta = \frac{N \times I}{3361\ \text{(constant)}}$$

where,

$\tan\theta$ = average angle of slope

N = average number of contour crossings per mile

I = contour interval in feet

For rainfall analysis hourly data of seven years has been collected from Indian Meteorological Department. Average hourly variation of rainfall during monsoon period (May to September) of a few consecutive years has been tabulated and calculated by the following formula:

$$R = \frac{r}{n}$$

where, R= average rainfall per hour

r = total rainfall of the hour of the month

and n = total number of rainfall occurrence of the hour of the month

In order to adopt a pragmatic approach, standard deviation and co-efficient of variations of hourly data have been calculated on the basis of the following formula :

$$\sigma = \sqrt{\frac{\Sigma(x-\overline{x})^2}{n}}$$

Where, σ = standard deviation
$\overline{x}$ = hourly rainfall
x = mean hourly rainfall
(i) n = number of observation

and (ii)

$$cv = \frac{\sigma}{\overline{x}} \times 100$$

where, cv = coefficient of variation of mean hourly rainfall
σ = standard deviation
$\overline{x}$ = mean hourly rainfall.

The data regarding various levels of water in Brahmaputra has been collected from Brahmaputra Flood Control Department for the monsoon period of 150 days (May to September), the average water level percentage of 150 days and cumulative percentage of 150 days has also been calculated.

This way most of the parameters have been analysed and presented with the help of suitable diagrams and other cartographic aids. A few secondary data relevant to the problems have also been collected from Town and Country Planning Department and Guwahati Municipal Corporation.

Results and Analysis

(a) *Average Slope Analysis*

The term slope is used for the land surface, which is inclined from the horizontal. The average slope of Greater Guwahati has been studied with the help of average slope determination of C.K. Wentworth.[2]

It is found that the average slope of Greater Guwahati varies from zero degree to 18 degrees. The maximum slope is 18 degrees and is noticed in the Nilachal Hill (6° to 18°), Kalapahar-Narakasur Hill (9° to 18°) and the Khanapara Hill side (6° to 18°) areas (Figure 7.1). In the same way Hengerabari N.C., Modgharia N.C., Ramcha Hill Grant, Sunsali Grant, Clearance Garden, Noonmati Garden, all are in the North-Eastern part of the Greater Guwahati, where the average slope varies from 9° to 18° or above. Both Kalapahar-Narakasur hill and Hengerabari-Modgharia hill area, the slope declines to 3 degrees near Ganeshguri. Beyond these areas the plains extend from Saukuchi, Sijubari, Hatigaon to Satgaon. A corridor of less than 3 degrees of average slope has been found between the westward slope of Nilachal Hills and the eastward slope of Jalukbari hill area. Further, it is noticed that the 3 degrees isopleth encircles the Dipar Beel and extends along the Pub-Bora Gaon to Borjhar-Azara area, here the western limit of the greater Guwahati ends. It is also observed that the Mora-Bharalu plains extend south to north between the Fatasil and Kalapahar hills. An isolated spot near Mikirpara, where slope increases for 3 to 6 degrees and another spot near Kakatipara where slope increases from 3 to 12 degrees, are found in the south west limit of Guwahati. These isolated hills are actually outliers of the Meghalaya Plateau.

The three tributary basins of Greater Guwahati are of contrasting characters. The Bondajan basin is found at higher altitude, having a 9 degree slope; Bharalu basin on 6 degree slope, while the Khanajan basin lies below 3 degree slope. Thus, it has been observed that the average slope of the urban complex gradually falls towards west, with exceptional inter-basin separation.

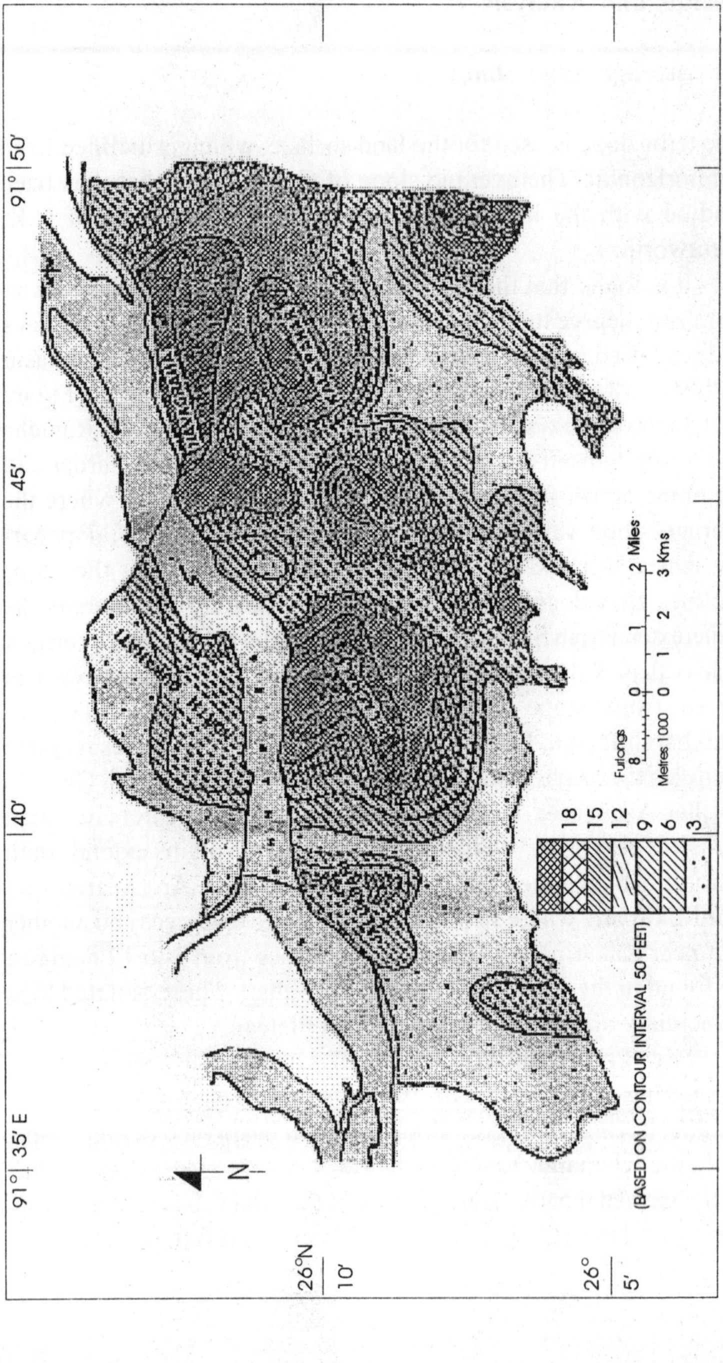

Fig. 7.1 : Guwahati: Average land Slope

The intervening hills, dividing the basins, are the residual outliers of the Maghalaya Plateau. These have been considerably eroded and demonstrate only relict monadnocks. The relief and slope characteristics of Greater Guwahati region indicate that while the natural inclination of the relief is from east to west, the drainage of the three tributaries to Brahmaputra has been at right angle to the natural inclination. Moreover, the orientation of the city is axial, along the Brahmaputra in east-west direction and the natural drainage courses again intersect the city at right angle and therefore, the natural courses have been intersected by roads, bridges, culverts and such other man-made hindrances.

(b) *Rainfall Analysis*

The water logging and inundation problems may be looked into from the point of view of rainfall intensity and rainfall regime of the city. Rainfall data for each hour for 7 years (1980-86) of 5 monsoon months (i.e. May to September) has been used and analysed. The average rainfall per hour for each monsoon months and for the season has been plotted in the graphs. The graphs are not smooth and show many primary and secondary peaks. To make the curve smooth three points moving average (Table 7.1) has been used. Yet some of the smoothed curves have shown oscillatory character (Fig. 7.2).

The May curve indicates few peaks, out of which, two are greater than the mean rainfall of 24 hours. May, June and July curves show prominent peaks. The characteristic feature of high peak of May 2300 hour IST corresponds to afternoon peak of July 1400 hour IST and then to early hour peak to July 0200 hour IST. The peaks are conspicuously smooth in the month of August. Significantly both early peak 0300 hour IST and late peaks 2000 to 2300 hour IST occur in September. During the monsoon season as a whole the rainfall curve shows three prominent peaks each at 2300 hour IST, 1400 hour IST and 0200 hour IST. Along with these three prominent peaks, there are five other mild peaks which are above mean rainfall. From the above analysis it is apparent that

Table 7.1 : Average Variation of Rainfall per hour for the Monsoon Season 1980-86*

(Rainfall in mm)

Hours	May	June	July	August	Sep-tember	Seasonal (monsoon)
1	2	3	4	5	6	7
1	3.9	3.7	3.4	3.2	3.6	3.6
2	5.0	3.0	6.5	2.9	2.0	3.9
3	3.1	2.7	3.4	3.4	5.5	3.6
4	3.3	2.1	1.3	1.2	3.0	2.2
5	2.9	1.9	1.7	4.0	1.7	2.4
6	1.7	1.5	1.9	4.4	1.1	2.1
7	3.0	1.2	2.1	3.3	1.0	2.1
8	1.2	1.0	2.1	3.1	2.7	2.0
9	2.5	2.1	2.9	3.4	1.6	2.5
10	1.5	2.6	2.6	3.0	1.5	2.2
11	1.8	3.0	3.1	2.3	2.0	2.4
12	1.6	4.3	1.9	2.5	2.3	2.5
13	1.7	3.4	1.1	2.6	1.5	2.0
14	1.2	10.0	1.2	1.4	1.1	3.0
15	2.9	1.7	1.6	1.8	1.9	2.0
16	1.0	5.8	1.3	2.5	1.7	2.5
17	1.2	5.0	4.6	2.4	3.3	3.3
18	2.1	1.4	1.5	3.7	1.4	2.0
19	2.6	1.3	2.3	1.9	2.2	2.0
20	2.8	2.0	2.4	2.1	4.1	2.7
21	1.4	2.0	5.1	4.1	4.5	3.4
22	3.0	5.1	2.4	3.2	3.0	3.3
23	8.8	1.8	3.3	2.2	4.0	4.0
24	4.8	2.2	2.7	2.5	2.0	2.8

* Computed by the author from the data of Indian Meteorological Department, Guwahati.

Guwahati experiences about eight peaks hours of high intensity rainfall periods in one monsoon season. The rainfall curve clearly depicts (Fig. 7.2) that most the rainfall occurred in afternoon and during night, whereas it is less between 0400 hour to 1300 hour IST.

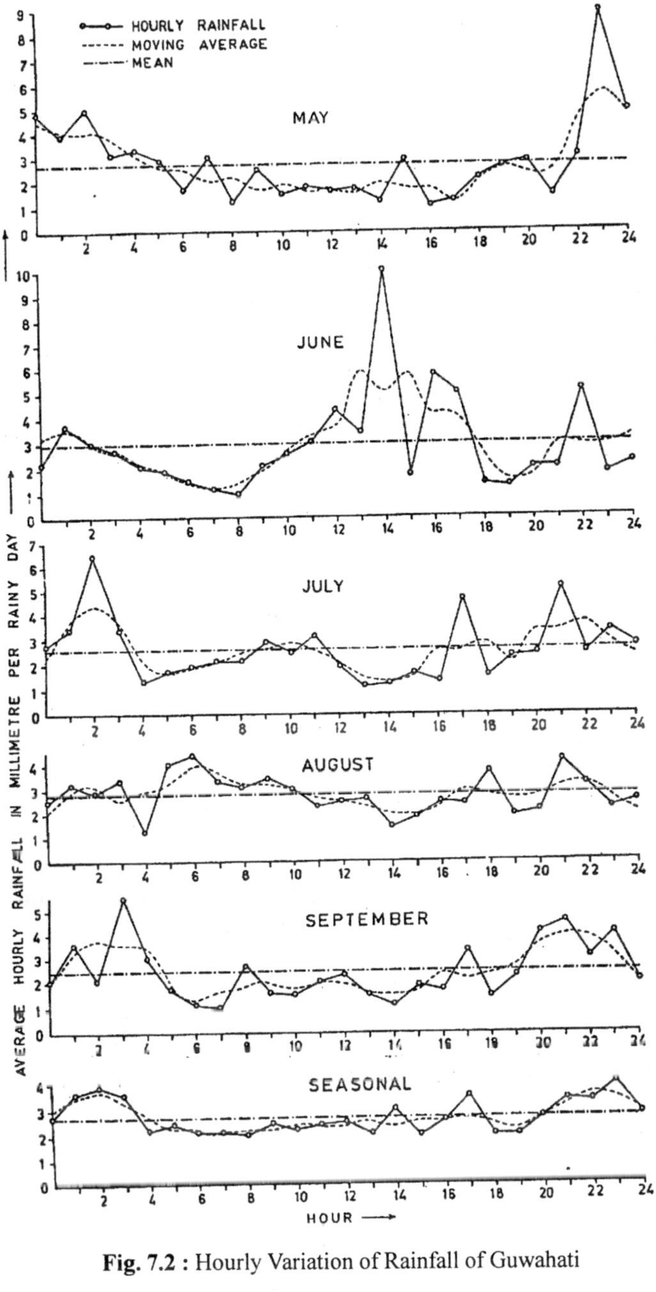

Fig. 7.2 : Hourly Variation of Rainfall of Guwahati

Table 7.2 : Three-Point Moving Average of Rainfall per hour for the Monsoon Season 1980-86*

(Rainfall in mm)

Three point moving average of the hours			May	June	July	Aug	Sep	Seasonal monsoon
1	2	3	4.0	3.1	4.4	3.1	3.7	3.7
2	3	4	3.8	2.6	3.7	2.5	3.5	3.2
3	4	5	3.1	2.2	2.1	2.9	3.4	2.7
4	5	6	2.6	1.8	1.6	3.2	1.9	2.2
5	6	7	2.5	1.5	1.9	3.9	1.3	2.2
6	7	8	2.0	1.2	2.0	3.6	1.6	2.1
7	8	9	2.2	1.4	2.4	3.2	1.8	2.2
8	9	10	1.7	1.9	2.5	3.1	1.9	2.2
9	10	11	1.9	2.6	2.8	2.9	1.7	2.4
10	11	12	1.6	3.3	2.5	2.6	1.9	2.3
11	12	13	1.7	3.5	2.0	2.5	1.9	2.5
12	13	14	1.5	5.9	1.4	2.2	1.6	2.3
13	14	15	1.9	5.0	1.3	1.9	1.5	2.5
14	15	16	1.7	5.8	1.4	1.3	1.6	2.6
15	16	17	1.7	4.1	2.5	2.2	2.3	2.6
16	17	18	1.1	4.0	2.5	2.9	2.1	2.4
17	18	19	2.0	2.5	2.8	2.7	2.3	2.2
18	19	20	2.5	1.5	2.0	2.6	2.6	2.7
19	20	21	2.3	1.7	3.3	2.7	3.6	3.1
20	21	22	2.4	3.0	3.3	3.1	3.9	3.6
21	22	23	4.4	2.9	3.6	3.2	3.8	3.4
22	23	24	5.5	3.0	2.8	2.6	3.0	3.4

*Computed by the author.

The means hourly rainfall per rainy day is maximum and becomes incessant in June and the minimum in September (Table 7.3). The co-efficient of variation of mean hourly rainfall is also maximum in June. Hence, June rainfall always alarming as soils absorbs by the rain water into the saturated point. The other peaks (primary and secondary maxima) from June to September, is a sensitive period with full of potential of flooding the city through runoff water.

Table 7.3 : Mean, Standard Deviation and Co-efficient of Variation of Rainfall per hour per Rainy Day for the Months of May to September and for the Season 1980-1986*

Months	Average hourly rainfall in mm ($\overline{x}$)	Standard Deviation of $\overline{x}$ (in mm)	Co-efficient of Variation of $\overline{x}$ in %
May	2.70	1.69	62.59
June	2.95	1.99	67.45
July	2.59	1.31	50.57
August	2.79	0.82	29.39
September	2.44	1.19	48.77
Seasonal (Monsoon)	2.68	0.66	24.62

* Computer by Author.

(c) *Behaviour of River water inside Greater Guwahati*

The tributaries of Brahmaputra inside Greater Guwahati are rendered inactive in discharging their water load because of the higher water level in the 'master drain'. On the contrary, backflow from the river Brahmaputra enters through the outlets of natural drainage and increases both the level and volume of water in these tributaries. Normally, backflow through Bondajan on the east, Khanajan on the west and Bharalu in the central part, causes flood inside Greater Guwahati almost at every spate of high water in Brahmaputra.

From the 10 years observations of the water level of Brahmaputra at D.C. Court site shows that the water level of Brahmaputra rises above the danger level (49.68 m.) seven times in ten years duration. It means that hardly one year was free from flood out of every three years.

Monthly water level of the Brahmaputra for D.C. court has been studied and it is plotted in the graph (Fig. 7.3). From this curve it is observed that the water level crossed the danger mark twice in 1980, once in 1981, thrice in 1987, and twice in 1985. In the year 1982,1983 and 1986 the water level did not cross the red mark (49.68 m) at all. The water level that crossing the danger level generally, in between July, August and September only.

An observation has been made on the daily water level of Brahmaputra at D.C.Court site for seven years and tabulated in

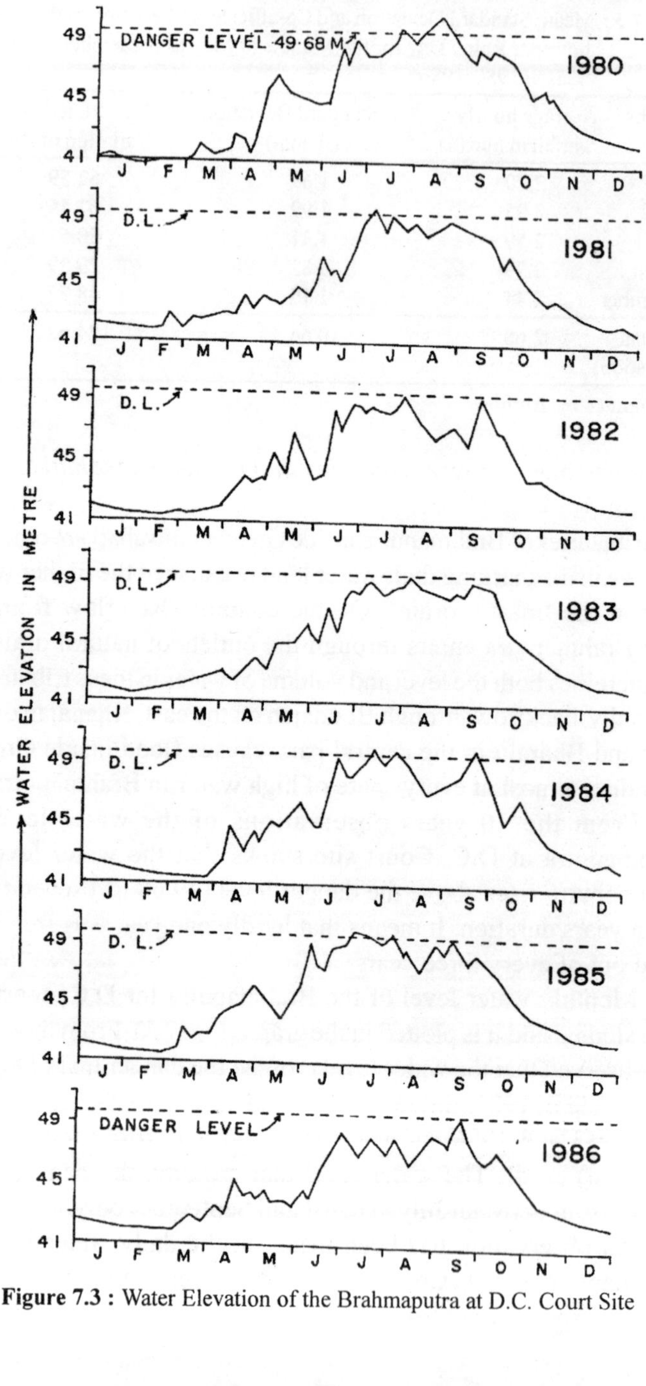

Figure 7.3 : Water Elevation of the Brahmaputra at D.C. Court Site

percentage (Table 7.4) for 150 days (May to September) and represented cumulative graph (Fig. 7.4) . It shows that for about 7 per cent of 150 days (10.5 days) the water level of Brahmaputra equals the danger level or exceeds it during the monsoon period. During this period when water level exceeds or equals the danger level, the sluice of Bharalu is to be closed to stop the back flow from the Brahmaputra in order to avoid inundation of the city area.

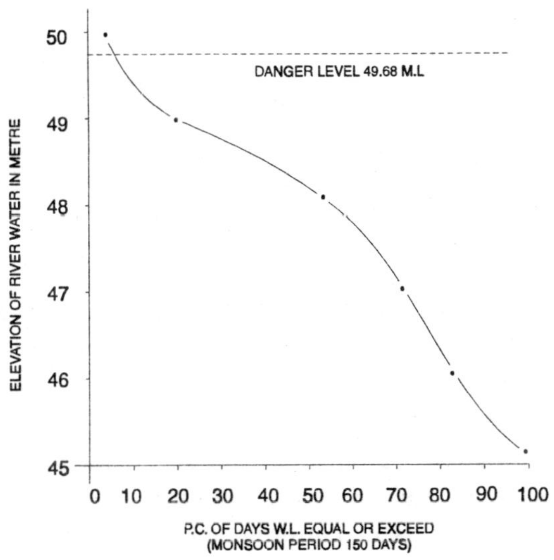

Fig. 7.4 : Water Level Duration Curve of the Brahmaputra at D.C. Court, 1980-86

"Gradient or slope of the stream channel is the angle between the water surface and the horizontal plane."[3] In general, a stream's gradient decreases from its source towards the month. But in case of the Bharalu river, the gradient of the river bed does fall progressively, but at certain meanders, the river bed is found to be of higher elevation than the upper course. This is mainly due to the sluggish movement of the water in the lean season and deposition of silt of the bed. This is another reason for rapid rise of water level in the river.

Table 7.4 : Number of Days the Water Level was above Mean Sea Level

Year	50m	49m	48m	47m	46m	45m
1980	8 days	27 days	65 days	13 days	5 days	32 days
1981	0 days	27 days	60 days	4 days	18 days	16 days
1982	0 days	14 days	50 days	25 days	27 days	10 days
1983	0 days	22 days	65 days	22 days	15 days	39 days
1984	10 days	37 days	35 days	31 days	28 days	40 days
1985	0 days	44 days	50 days	36 days	6 days	17 days
1986	0 days	6 days	33 days	59 days	32 days	7 days
Total	18 days	117 days	258 days	190 days	131 days	161 days
Average days	2.6	25.3	51.1	27.1	18.7	23.0
% of 150 days	1.7	16.8	34.1	18.1	12.5	15.3
Cumulative	1.7	18.5	52.6	70.7	82.2	100

Source : Above data computed by the author from Brahmaputra Flood Control Commission, Guwahati.

Note : At D.C. Court danger level is 49.68 m.

The closure of the sluice gate near the Pragjyotish College results in accumulation of the rainwater from the catchment area in the drain. As this water cannot flow out through its mouth at the time of high water in Brahmaputra, the accumulated water takes a reverse course and slowly drains out through the Mora-Bharalu (dead river) to Dipar Beel. Unfortunately, the shallow and narrow channel of Mora-Bharalu fails to clear off the accumulated water with any great speed. This keeps the water level of the Bharalu river high for weeks together and causes water logging in the entire low-lying areas of the basin.

(d) *Waterlogging and Inundation Problems*

Waterlogging is a colossal and continuous problem of Guwahati. In order to locate and verify the vulnerable waterlogging spots, constant personal observation was made by the researcher in the last few consecutive monsoons. Empirically speaking, few causes may be attributed to this phenomenon:

(i) Topography of Guwahati is singnificantly undulating.
(ii) Both natural and artificial drains are not capable of carrying the storm water due to their shallowness and narrowness.
(iii) Encroachments over the low-lying areas by new settlers on either side of the natural drains have blocked the natural flow of flood water to the drains.
(iv) Construction of building and roads over the man-made drains are also responsible for bottlenecking the drainage.
(v) Indiscriminate cutting of hill sides for filling up low-lying areas are also responsible for sheet wash and blockage of channels. The hills are exposed to heavy rain which supply enormous loose soil and silt up the drains rapidly.
(vi) The filled-up areas possess high seepage capacity because of lower compactness and saturate at a faster rate and therefore, do not allow flow of flood water.
(vii) Most of the original swamps and natural water reservoirs are filled up for residential, official, industrial and institutional purposes. Consequently, the rain water spread over the built-up areas causing flash flood.
(viii) Rising of the ground water table with the rise of Brahmaputra level saturates the entire plain area and reduces the rate of percolation.

The topography of Guwahati controls the natural drainage. As mentioned earlier. The relief of the city gradually slopes from east to west. Two major natural drains of Greater Guwahati originate in the hills and other two major drains originate from lakes. Mushrooming of settlements on either sides of the perennials drains in and around Guwahati restrict easy flow of water. In between the natural drains, the presence of depressed area usually prompt the tendency of collection of water in scattered areas after every heavy shower.

The cultural morphology of the city has undergone tremendous change and new settlements particularly, the unplanned ones have created many bottlenecks to the system of natural drainage. Within the busy functional areas of the city, drain-cum-footpaths are not adequate to carry all the storm waters. Besides, most of the drains are relentlessly constructed against the natural direction of flow.

In addition, the broad gauge railway line has been constructed through the heart of the city, which constrains the existing inadequate drainage system of the city. Ignoring the Master Plan of the city and construction of broad gauge line across the natural courses have added to the problem.

Enormous sheet wash from Navagraha hill slopes constantly fill up the existing drains and flood the road from Silpukhuri to the Flood Control Commission Office at Chandmari. Similar situations are also seen over the road near Assam Engineering Institute to Bamunimaidan area.

In matters of water logging, the composition of the soil in the city area has a major role to play. At one hand, the depressed area are composed of transported soil from the hilly areas and at the other, much of the built-up areas have come up over the newly field soils. The rain-water, in absence of effective soil conserving cover, erode the high land and deposit the materials over the low-lying areas. The water percolation rate reached the lowest point during the monsoon period. Two specific reasons may be attributed to this phenomenon :

(i) The low-lying areas are composed of transported soil or silt,

(ii) Widespread saturation of the soil takes place as noted earlier, due to rise of Brahmaputra level and due to the nature of its soil composition. Consequently, the surface flow progressively increases with the advance of monsoon season, resulting in the collection of rain-water in the depressed regions. The best example of such a situation may be cited from Kumarpara area. The elevation of this area is comparatively low (49 m above MSL, whereas, danger level of Brahmaputra is 49.68 m at D.C. Court site). Being nearer to the Brahmaputra and the Bharalu, soil of the area gets rapidly saturated with the advent of monsoon. The sub-soil of this region hardly gets time for complete desiccation in between the wet seasons and the monsoon, coupled with high water in the Brahmaputra, completely stops percolation. Hence, the entire Kumarpara area is submerged during heavy showers.

Illegal encroachers fill up most of the natural water reservoirs of Greater Guwahati. The swampy areas in between Fatasil and Lakhra road are packed with settlements. The Bishnupur area, and the low-lying areas of Gopinath Nagar are also filled up for construction of residential quarters, resulting in permanent blockade of rain-water. The areas in between the Rajgarh Road and R.G. Baruah Road significantly, lies below 49 m contour. This part of the city is also subjected to continuous earth filling for new constructions of residential houses. In the absence of effective outlets, the water in unfilled areas remains stagnant causing water-logging for weeks together.

Looking into the growth momentum of the city, establishment of industrial areas and capital complex in and around the city, various government agencies have offered suggestion for alleviation of this problem. The notable suggestions offered by the Town Planning Organisation, Assam, and the Brahmaputra Flood Control Board perhaps, would ease the situation to a certain extent, provided these schemes are effectively implemented. Nevertheless, it seems that the problem will persist for a long time to come without a long run plan of drainage of the city to be undertaken in a war footing.

Conclusions

The above analysis of various aspects of the city environs boils down to the following issues: These are– (a) the natural drainage problems, (b) the artificial drainage problems, and (c) the silting problems.

(a) *The Natural Drainage Problems*

The main natural drainage of the city is the Bharalu river. Prolonged silting and encroachment upon its banks have reduced the load discharge capacity of the drain, especially in the lower part from

R.G. Baruah Road bridge (Zoo Road bridge) to Lakhra Road bridge point.

Bed of the middle part of Mora-Bharalu is at a higher elevation, which fails to carry off the normal discharge. At the time of high water level of the Brahmaputra, the water back-flows into the city through the existing channels and open culverts. Dipar Beel needs to be excavated to enable it to absorb the city runoff through the existing drain. Barchala Beel connected through open drains cannot accommodate all the water received at the time of peak discharge. There is also no practical use of Chala Beel (Chatribari swamp) due to its shallowness. Hence, both the beels needs to be excavated to enable them to reserve the excess storm water.

(b) *The Artificial Drainage Problems*

Existing drainage facilities of Guwahati are not a adequate to carry all storm water from each of the localities. Hence, some more new drains could be constructed along the natural slope of the area. Moreover, existing drains can be renovated for easy flow of rainwater with provision of annual clearance.

As most of the roads, inside the city are very narrow, underground drains are desirable. These roads should not be utilised for drain-cum-footpath indiscriminately.

Existing manholes of drain-cum-footpaths are not adequate. More manholes and inlet holes are require for the quick disposal of silt and stagnated water. The size of the inlet holes and their position need to be re-oriented.

(c) *The Silting Problems*

The problem of silting is very serious, especially in high rainfall intensity areas, as it is related with the hill cutting and earth filling. Even, well-designed drainage systems may not cope up with the huge volume of silt load carried along with the runoff, unless some remedial measures are undertaken.

It is seen that clearing silt from the existing drains do not help as the high intensity of rainfall from surrounding hills with silt overflow towards the city dwellers. For this, deep drain may be constructed along foothills of all the hills located in and around Guwahati. Tunnel like drains should be constructed through Nilachal, Navagraha hills connecting drains of foothills to outlet it to the master drain Brahmaputra so that runoff with silt would be released immediately. Same way a few more 'silt traps' may be constructed important site along foothills of Sarania hills, Kalapahar, Narakasur, Fatasil, Sonaighul and Ramcha hills etc. These silt traps need to be cleaned after each storm. For this special labour force should be employed therein.

Before making any remedial measures for construction of drain, tunnel and silt traps, aerial photographs of two seasons of Greater Guwahati should be obtained. An aerial photograph covering water logging area of summer season and another aerial photograph of winter season should be obtained so that construction work could be aligned as per need in plan manner.

This work cannot be claimed to be all-pervading and complete in all aspects. There are ample scopes for further investigation in this field by experts. However, the contribution made through this humble work might be helpful in tackling this age-old problem.

References

1. A report on "Master Plan for Water Supply, Sewerage and Drainage" for Gauhati Metropolitan District; 1971-2001, recommended by Calcutta Metropolitan Planning Organisation, 1971.

2. Wentworth, C.K, 1930, "A simplified method of determining the average slope of land surface". *American Journal of Science*, vol. 220.

3. Strahler, A. N., 1971, *Physical Geography*, Willey Eastern Pvt. Ltd., New Delhi.

8

THE INCREASING SEWAGE AND INUNDATION PROBLEMS OF GUWAHATI CITY
A Perspective on Environmental Geography

M. Kar

Introduction

Urbanisation is the sign of development of modern world. Being an administrative, industrial and commercial centre, Guwahati is also considered as one of the fast growing urban units of India and therefore additional peoples are always tending to concentrated in the city. This city lies on a general flat plain with scattered pre-cambrian hills which are mainly made of granitic rocks. The ever increasing rate of urbanisation in the city has accelerated the amount of water discharge. On the other hand, with the increasing number of population, the rate of impervious surface is also increasing which in turn is reducing the rate of infiltration day by day. The existing drains in the city are found to be quite inadequate to drain out all the dischargeable waters and as a result tne city has to witness high amount of water logging specially during the rainy season. Works on this line has been done in the international level by Wolman (1967), Hammer (1972), Hollis and Luckett (1976), Leopold (1973), Fox (1976), Neller (1988), Knight (1979) and Kar (1993 and 1996).

Methodology

The study is based on primary datas, survey works and long data base of the last forty years has been considered. Hydrological, Meteorological and Geological parameters have also been considered in the course of study. In addition to this, the empirical methodologies and statistical techniques along with models are used for better understanding. Moreover, computerised analysis are also done for more accuracy and laboratory data management.

Analysis

Guwahati city is one of the fast growing urban centres having been known as the gateway of North-East India. The city area does not present a smooth land and some variation can be noticed in almost all the parts of the city. Most of the areas of the city are found to be composed of resistant igneous and metamorphic rocks, with little alluvium soils scattered all over the region (Map 8.1)

The expansion of the urban landscape has achieved a remarkable development specially after 1947 and the present expansion of the city is the result of the agglomeration of the urban structure developed around a multiple nuclei. Since 1947, numerous achievements were made specially in the field of social, economic and cultural needs of the city, as a result of which many government and non-governmental institutions of national and provincial importance had come into existence. Moreover, with the shifting of the state capital from Shillong to Guwahati and also with the migration of several foreign nationals specially from Bangladesh (earstwhile Pakistan), there has been a considerable rise in the rate of population in the city.

On the other hand with the ever-increasing stream of men from various parts of the country mainly in search of employment has also rendered a spectacular growth of urban population. In addition to this, by the introduction of the Night Super Buses and the Inter-city train services, there has also been a remarkable rise mainly in the amount of floating population in the city. It has been estimated that everyday an average of 10% extra population intrudes

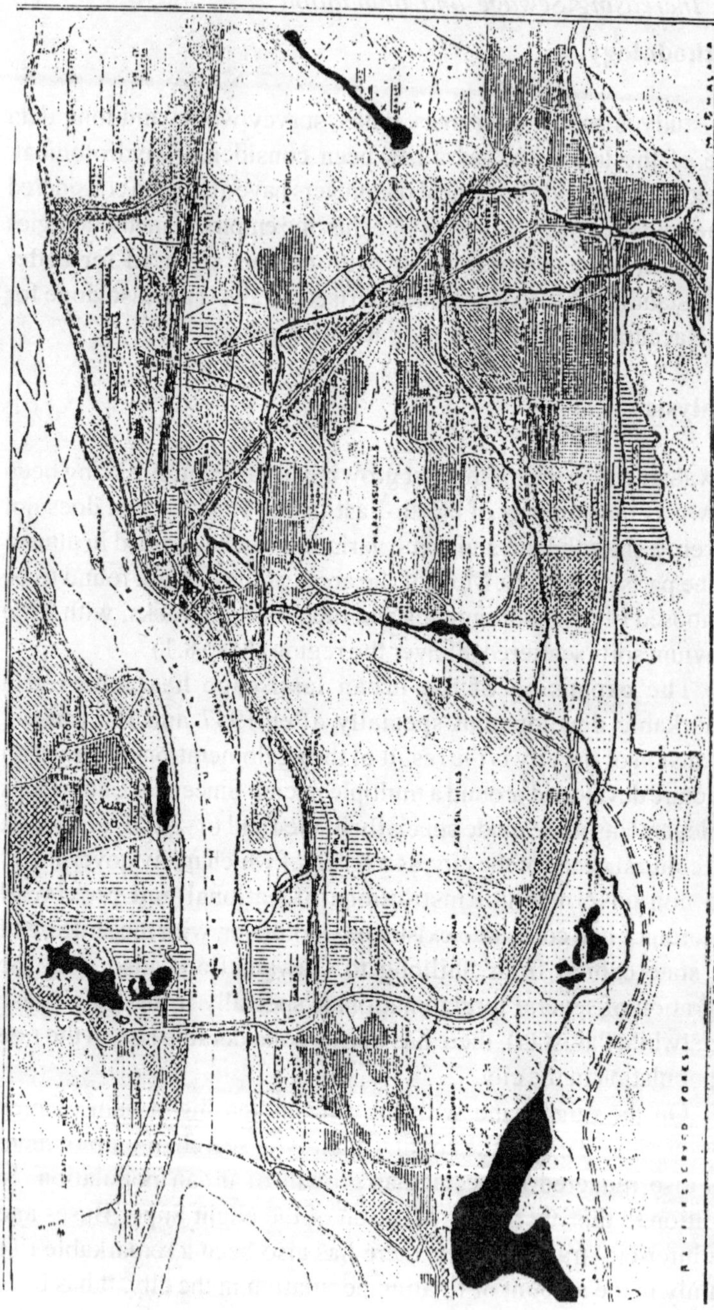

Map 8.1 : Guwahati

into the city area which increases another 1.2 lakhs of population.

This phenomenal growth of population had lead the Guwahati Municipality to extend its boundary by introducing new wards, which started from 1961 having 14.24 sq. kms. Today the actual area of Guwahati city is more than 44.00 sq. kms and the area under G.M.C. is about 215.73 sq. kms. as defined in the year 1971 which has further extended upto 259.07 sq. kms. in the year 1991 (Map 8.2). The total population under the G.M.C. area as shown in 1991 census was 5,89,342 persons.

The growing population in the city stressed the need for the expansion of new built up areas. In order to support this bulk of population, the new built up areas in the city zone increased to about 97.14% until the year 1961 with inclusion of new areas like Chandmari, Panbazar, Panchali, Bharalumukh, Santipur and Athgaon etc. This figure further rosed to 157:51% until 1991 with newly inhabited areas like Dispur, Basistha, Kahilipara, Beltola, Fatashil (Ambari), Kamakhya Gate, Maligaon, Durgasarubar and Six-Mile etc. being included under the G.M.E. (Fig. 8.1)

This gigantic concentration of population and expansion of built up areas has created the problem of garbage disposal, increase of sewerages and the problem of water logging in most parts of the city. The main reason for this is that, the city authority fails to introduce marks in proper drainage system. Although one can see several scattered swamps, marshers, water ponds and small streams with meandering courses mainly in the East and South of the city (Map 8.3), they cannot be considered as adequate to absorb all the foul waters emitted. Moreover, most of the low-lying plains in the city gets inundated at the time of high floods of the Brahmaputra river, because the gradients of these small streams are quite low and the flood water enter through these low-lying areas and adversely effects the present drainage and the sewerage systems in the city, only through the Bharalu near Pragjyotish College, which is to be renovated (Kar 1978, 1993).

In fact, the Brahmaputra and the Bharalu rivers are the only two natural drainage systems of the city excluding the Bonda and the Khanazan rivers. The Bharalu is in fact a small tributary of the Brahmaputra, which runs from South-East to North-East and afier attaining a sharp bend near the Fatashil hills, it flows towards the North and ultimately merges into the river Brahmaputra. In addition to this network, almost all the important sewers of the city are directly or indirectly connected with the Brahmaputra river.

During 1971, there were altogether 100 kms. of sewers in the city against 931 persons per sq. kms. Although figure had increased upto 1,300 kms. during 1991, yet they are not adequate to carry out the foul water released because the population density in the city also increased upto 33,359 persons per sq. km. during the same year. The relation between the unproportional nature of the length of the sewers in relation to the size of population during these two years is shown in (Fig. 8.2).

From our study, it is found that during the last two decades, Guwahati has spreads from its nucleus site to the countryside and is expanding at a vertical scale.

This present three-dimensional structure of the city supports a large number of population which in turn is releasing foul water and sewage thrice the amount of the existing sewers. The result is that most of the sewers, owing to its smaller size (0.3–1.2 m of width) and (0.3 – 1.3 of depth), cannot carry out the load and generally over flows to its bank resulting in large scale water logging mainly in the low-lying areas of Manik Nagar, Krishna Nagar, Sundarpur, Zoo Road, parts of Hatigaon, Christian Basti, Nitamoni Phukan Road, Chandmari, Lakhtokia, Machkhowa and Santipur.

Yet another cause for the problem of water logging in the city is the large scale rate of siltation mainly in the sewers. The main reason for the increasing nature in the rate of siltation can be traced out as the resulting factor of rapid earth cutting. Since early 1990, earth cutting in the hill slopes has become an issue and regular increase in the amount of siltation became a serious threat to the Guwahati Municipal Corporation. Our study reveals that, at present most of the sewers in the city are loaded with 0.5-1.0 m. of silt bed, which is reducing the carrying capacity of the sewers and resulting in large scale water loggings. This condition can be experienced in

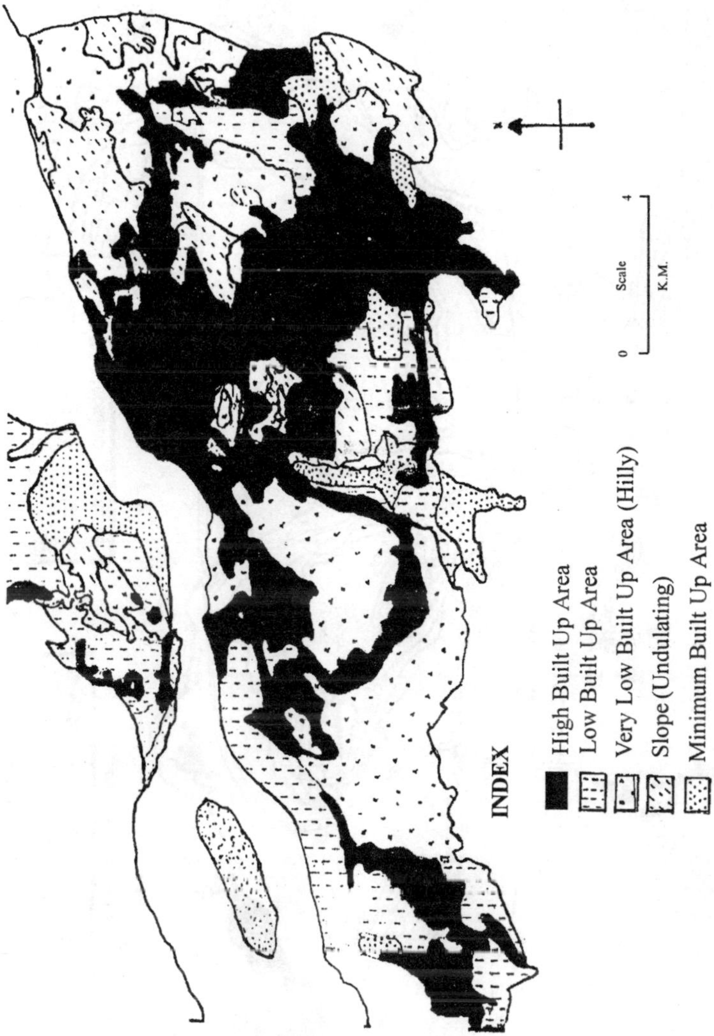

Map 8.2 : Map showing the built up area of Guwahati city.

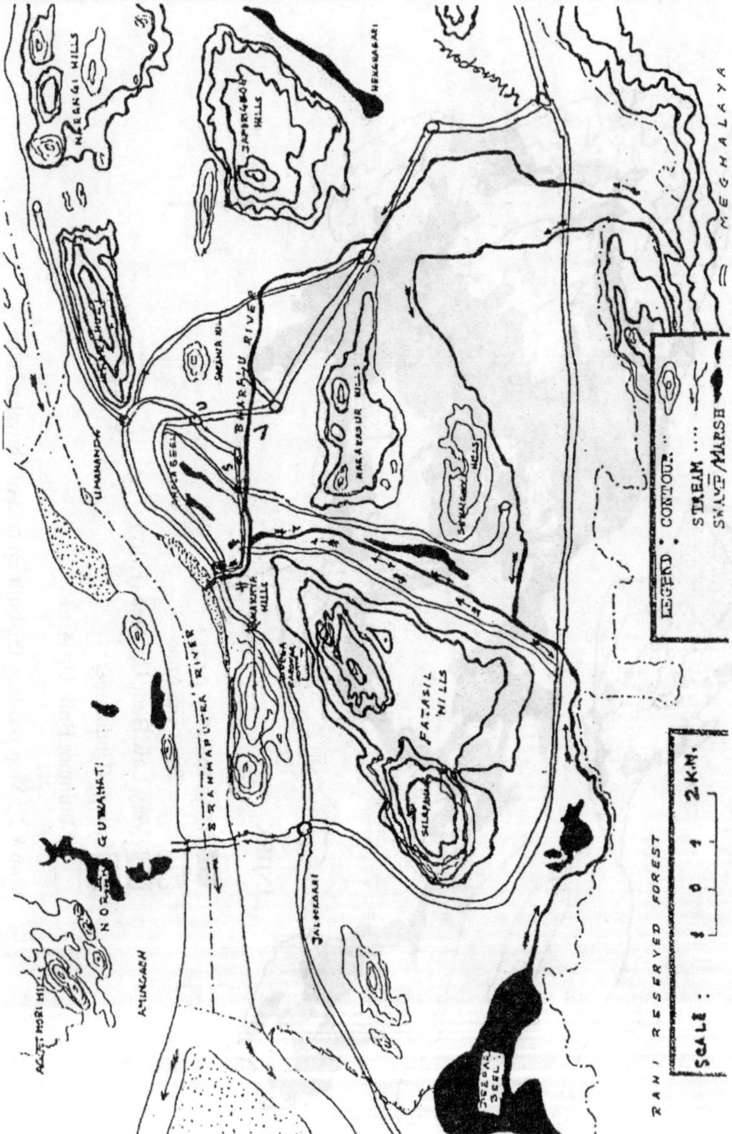

Map 8.3 : Guwahati Map showing the Natural Drainage Systems.

the areas of Japorigog, Zoo Tinali, Chandmari, Bamunimaidam and Silpukhuri respectively.

The study also reveals that the Narakashur hills, the Fatashil hills, Silapahar and the Japarigog hills had lost its previous ecological conditions. Upto 1970, there were innumerable springs and forest species. But now the forests are disappearing rapidly in these areas with bare hills all over, which has lead to the destruction of many important floras and faunas, generally providing essential nutrients and humus to soil.

Water has the property of dissolving and carrying in solution a variety of chemicals and other matters. In this process it gets contaminated and becomes a threat to men and other living organism. It is found from our study that the amount of contaminated ground water is increasing in the city mainly because of the large scale use of toxic chemicals. Pesticides, herbicides, hazardous substances and the rapid use of plastic goods. Therefore, an urgent need for monitoring the different level of water pollution. Now our demand for drinking water and other purposes are also constantly on the increase. This adds to the volume of sewerages and also contaminates other potential supplies. Thus, the ground water management should come forward with advanced techniques to develop the ground water resources. These calls for a clear understanding of the hydrological aspects of the area and a co-ordinated approach is greatly needed by the planners, hydrologists, irrigation engineers and the social scientists.

Some Measures

The following steps are to be adopted strictly by the planners to control the increasing nature of the drains and the inundation problems in the city.

(1) The earth cutting in the hill slopes should be stopped immediately.

This will reduce the problem of soil erosion and the rate of siltation in the drains.

(2) Preferences should be given more in constructing houses generally erected on plinths. Some 2-3 feet above the ground (*Chang Ghar*) mainly in the hill slopes.

This will keep the hill slopes unaffected.

(3) Efforts should be made to convert the existing drains free from garbage.

This will increase the water carrying capacity of the drains and the problem of waterlogging will be reduced.

(4) Installation of Ring Culverts should be abolished.

This generally reduce the water carrying capacity.

(5) Proper maintenance of the drains should be done immediately after the rainy season.

This will expand the life of the drain in the city.

(6) Non-degradable solid wastes like plastics, polythenes, rubbers and metals etc. should not be thrown into the drains.

These wastes generally act as garbage stores in the drains and hinders the movement of the sewerages.

(7) The existing drains should be expanded in every five to ten years interval.

This will reduce the problem of waterlogging in the low-lying areas of the city.

(8) The foul waters should be stored in underground tanks as far as possible.

This will recharge the soil and the ground water level.

(9) The rain water should be stored at the top of buildings during the time of showers.

The water should only be released in accordance to the city water commission's instructions.

This will reduce the extra load in the drains during the showers and will result in the decrease of waterlogging.

(10) The Bharalu river system should be protected in all cost. This is the lifeline of Guwahati City. This system only can solve the drainage problem alone. It is a unique drainage system in Guwahati city.

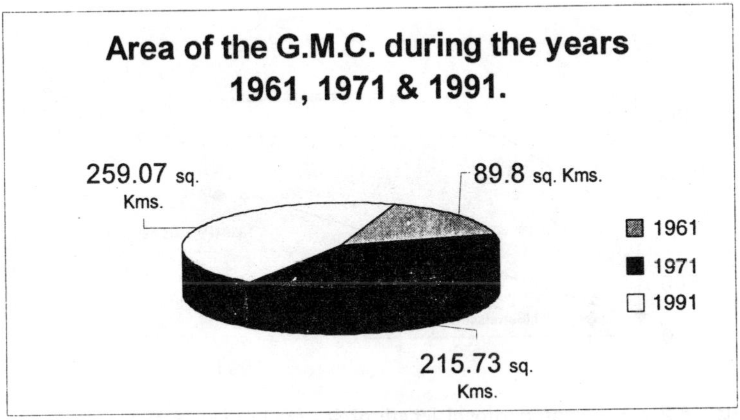
Area of the G.M.C. during the years
1961, 1971 & 1991.
259.07 sq. Kms.
89.8 sq. Kms.
215.73 sq. Kms.
1961
1971
1991

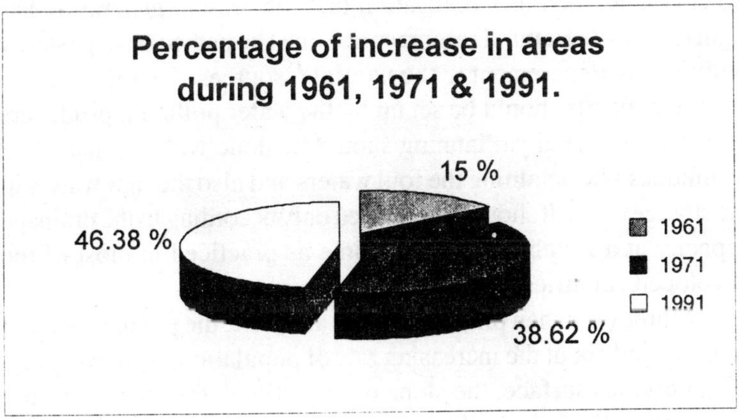
Percentage of increase in areas
during 1961, 1971 & 1991.
15 %
46.38 %
38.62 %
1961
1971
1991

Fig. 8.1

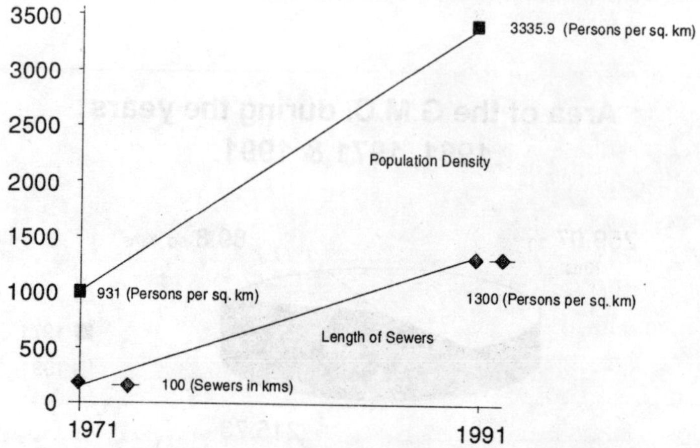

Fig. 8.2 : The unproportional length of sewers in relation to the density of population in Guwahati City in the year of 1971 & 1991.

Conclusion

To conclude, there is a realisation that the present generation has right to enjoy the natural resources and must be passed on to posterity without any imparement to the natural resources. Therefore, more treatment plants should be set up by the water pollutant producers industries in the city. Planning should be done with sophisticated techniques like detaining the foul waters and also the rain waters in the storage tanks. It should be released only according to the drainage capacity at a suitable interval of time as practiced in most of the developed countries of the world.

Moreover, when planning works are done, the planners should bear in mind about the increasing rate of population, increasing rate of impervious surface, the slope of the ground, the soil condition, the meteorological condition and also the nature of industrial expansion. Only in doing so, a final solution can come out and the sewerage system and hence the inundation problem in the city area can be solved.

References

Buttmer, M. Csillag, F. and Mather, P.M. (1998) : Spectural and spatial information content of SPOT Data. Proceedings of IGRASS '88 symposium. Edinburgh. UK (Vol. 1) pp. 211-212.

Bhattacharya, N. N. (1971), *Trends of Urbanization in Assam*, pp. 25-36.

Fox, H. I. (1976), The urbanizing river : A case study in the Maryland Peidmont, in D. R. Coats, (ed.), *Geomorphology and Engineering*, George Allen and Unwin, pp. 245-71.

Hammer, T. R., (1972), Stream Channel enlargement due to urbanization, *Water Resources Research* 8 pp. 1530-40.

Hollish, G. E. and Uckett, J, K, (1976) : The response of natural stream channels to urbanization : Two case studies from South-East England, *J. Hydrol.* 30, pp. 351-63.

Kar, M., (1978). *Proper Guwahati : Student Geographical Forum*, Gauhati University. Vol. 1, pp. 15-21.

Kar, M., (1982), Pollution of Natural Environment, *News Star*, A National Daily, Guwahati, Vol. 1, No. 123.

Kar, M., (1993), Guwahati : The two in one city, *The North-East Times*, July 18, Guwahati, Assam.

Kar, M.,(1996): A study of Drainage and Sewerage of Nagaon Town: A perspective of Engineering Geography, Earth Resource Management, Technical Paper, XVI International Congress, INCA in Indian Institute of Technology (IIT), New Delhi, Vol 16, pp. 307-10.

Knight, C.R.(1979), Urbanisation and Natural Stream channel morphology:The case of two English New Towns, in G.E. Hollis(etd). *Man's Impact on the Hydrological cycle in the United Kingdom*, Geobooks. pp.181-98.

Neller, R.J.(1988), a comparison of channel erosion in small Urban and rural catchments Armidale, New South Wales, *Earth Surface Processes and Landforms*, 13, p.1-7.

Pathan, S.K. Jothimani, P. Som, N.N. and Mukherjee, K.(1991): *Urban landuse studies of Calcutta.* ISRO, Ahemdabad and CMD Authority, Calcutta.

UNESCO (1979), Impact of urbanisation and industrialisation on water resources planning and management, Report of the UNESCO/HIP Workshop at Zandvoori, The Netherlands, (1977), UNESCO.

Wolman M.G.,(1967), A Cycle of Sedimentation and Erosion in urban river channels. *Geografiska Annaler*, 49, Series A pp. 385-95.

9

GUWAHATI MUNICIPAL PROBLEMS

S. Br. Medhi

With the shifting of capital of Assam from Shillong to Dispur in 1972, the cost of Guwahati land increased, water became scarce, drainage became a headache, roads got congested and security became a matter of great concern.

MAJOR PROBLEMS

While talking about the problems of Guwahati, I like to state that all the 92 towns of Assam have similar problems. One may go to Silchar or Dhubri and find out what is the state of affair. I like to note some of the major problems only from my practical experiences.

Roads

Our municipal roads are characterised by pot holes and narrowness– not to speak of the quality of footpaths. In fact, when I was in the State Human Rights Commission – we started cases against the Guwahati Municipal Corporation for footpath injury to some eminent citizens. Many places in the city need overbridges – but these are still undecided. In many places road/street lights are only for show just due to carelessness of the switchmen.

Flooding of roads are familiar picture. Experts say that every year the Brahmaputra is rising by about two inches and the depth of the river bed is being reduced. This problem can be solved by dredging the river. But I have not found anyone in Dispur writing any letter to the Dredging Corporation of India, HQ Visakhapatnam (AP) for any scheme.

Along with the floods come the drainage problem and we find faulty drainage spoils the road/street in any place. I found in the media recently that HUDCO sanctioned a loan of Rs.67 crores for a drainage scheme of GMDA (Guwahati city) to be started this year. But here the main question is – how effectively we coordinate the works of several departments such as of PWD, TCP Deptt., Flood Control Departments etc., and what is the efficiency/ effectiveness of GMDA as the model Agency for this scheme. This scheme involves improvement of Bharalu and Mora Bharalu rivers and shifting of sluice gate near Pragjyotish College, digging up of the bed of the river Bharalu etc. Again to reduce the water logging problem of GNB Road – GMDA has a plan for a drain costing about Rs. 43 lakhs. There are also plans for new drains or improvement of existing drains in several areas such as Santipur – Durgasarobar, Kumarpara, Lachitnagar, Hatigaon etc. GMDA also mentioned about construction of SILT CHAMBERS to reduce siltation of drains. In fact, irregular cleanings of drains in Guwahati is a rare event today.

While talking of roads – congestion is another problem. In UK, USA, USSR (Old) etc. we find railways coming underground while entering city and much of the traffic congestion is reduced by this technique. But this is not to be seen in our country as yet. Road side garrages and gas cylinder shops are adding to the gravity of this problem.

Many other facing problems on road also due to several factors such as – improper/defective police signals (owing to untrained traffic staff), high–speed city buses, big–sized buses and last of all

–the VIP traffic/cars travelling at 80 to 100 kms. per hour without caring for safety of others on the road.

Water

Coming to the quantitative aspect – we find that we do not get sufficient drinking water in any part of the city/town. No doubt production is below demand level but I find that whatever is produced (for drinking) is also not distributed properly. No doubt old pumps of Satpukhuri (Riverside – near Belle Vue Hotel) are useless but there is no effort to replace these. I found on my survey trip that the old pumps cannot lift water to hill – to reservoirs as per standard. Secondly, the leakage in the tanks result in loss of about 25 per cent water in one hour or so. Thirdly, the water main pumps are damaged (by traffic or by anti-social elements for unauthorised connections) at several places. As much water is lost on the way in transit before reaching the house of the consumers/tax-payers. What is more frustrating — even today we find many public free drinking water taps all over the city. And the people get water although they do not pay-taxes. At the same time these free takers do not close the taps after taking water. Our precious water is lost in this way to the tune of about 25 per cent of the total production as per one estimate. Can we not have water meter as in W. War-II days?

Regarding the qualitative aspect – I found in my survey that there were no covers in many tanks all over the city. In many places these were removed by nearby people to syphone off water for their private use secretly. There is also no regular cleaning of these tanks. Normally, the date of cleaning should be written in bold letters outside the tank wall for notice of anyone . It is unfortunate to note that no senior officer visits the tanks or leaking pipes for corrective actions. And the key operators – being 4th grade staff do not take initiative for rectifying these defects – in tanks or main pipes. I found similar problems in the activities of the Assam Urban Water Supply & Sewerage Board (AUWSSB) – a state Public Sector Enterprise set up in 1989 – to provide safe water and scientific sewerage system in all urban areas of Assam. This PSU also has not been able to have a Master Plan for drainage and disposal of sewerage in Greater Guwahati in collaboration with GMC and GMDA. There are too many organisations and too little action for giving relief to the people in time. About 20 water schemes were started by the AUWSSB but they could not answer properly when I asked them details of these schemes (and amount spent) in the meetings of the Board of Directors as I was also one of the Directors. The accounts of the AUWSSB are not updated for several years despite my warnings. We have not got returns for our public/tax money spent on these schemes for several years – mainly due to mismanagement. And mismanagement occurs when wrong persons are posted on political pressures.

Pollution

Today, countries like Namibia and Mongolia have cleaner atmosphere than India. We are familiar with air and noise pollution in Guwahati. There are more than 125 defective city buses (engine) in this city. Solid waste management has become our new problem with growing population. With the growth of NURSING HOMES – toxic and hazardous waste disposal and discharges have become a headache. Till now, we have no Acts to control these activities. Burning of firewood, coal etc. are not yet banned. Of course, gas cylinders are not available to everyone. But then why cannot we press the Authorities to start GAS PIPELINES connections to every home as in Sibsagar, Dibrugarh town etc. Today even many parts of greater Bombay and Calcutta have such gas pipelines – which have greatly helped controlling air pollution.

It may be noted here we in the Human Rights Commission tried to control air pollution due to vehicles emissions and issued notices to all connected departments like – Transport, Civil Supplies, GMC etc. but it appears there is no seriousness to start mobile/small POL testing centres at selected POL depots as in Delhi and other big cities.

Pollution due to waterlogging is well known in this city. Recently the Government of India had written to all Chief Secretaries to prepare schemes for better waste water management. Calcutta has planned safe disposal of waste water. We have learnt from Ganga Action Plan (WB) that many conventional sewage treatment plants have high operation and maintenance costs and these also do not reduce the level of bacteria to the permissible limit. GMC should note that now the Central Government is giving finance for setting up Water Tanks for waste water treatment.

Pollution control is important for health reasons as we find several examples in the World Bank Report of 1999; it is stated that in South Asia 20 percent of total burden of disease is due to environmental causes – over half from diarrhoeal diseases and lack of water and sanitation.

Sanitation

While discussing this aspect – I recall how the Central Government started schemes for health care and slaughter houses and public toilets and permanent dustbins etc. What have we done in Assam in 1999? I found very bad management of HUDCO money by Housing Board of Assam in public toilet schemes in various towns of Assam – while I was the MAD Secretary. Why no massive tree planting schemes in city areas – by Government or through NGOs. In Sanghinagar (near Hyderabad) I found a barren hill turned to a green refreshing area with very little cost. Can we not learn from such lessons?

Security

The cumulative effect is – we have no security and no peace of mind in the municipal area – not to speak of peace and security in villages and uncared areas in this 21st century. What are we doing about landslides and earthquake-prone areas and fire-fighting techniques in city area? What about careless Gas Cylinder distribution points? Why crime and violence will not increase when police outposts are not located properly in needy areas? Why the Jail is not shifted to a safer place from the crowded bazar area of Fancy

Bazar? Recently, I visited the new Central Jail at Maulal (about 25 kms from Hyderabad) are learnt why the old Nizam's Jail is shifted from crowded area of Hyderabad to Maulali. It is better than any University and it has everything including a high-tech operation theatre constructed at a cost of Rs. 50 crores in just one year time.

SOLUTIONS

1. In my opinion, fund is not the problem. We have perverse budget priorities and we have mismanaged since 1947. Today the NGOs and private sector are solving problems in Madras, Ahmedabad and Baroda. We have also seen new techniques like BOT, Bond Market, Debt Market etc. for finance. Many services can be privatised-especially in Parks, Garbage disposal etc. and even in Tax collection. We can also get donations or works from corporate sector. What is needed is Dynamic Management.

Moreover, International Agencies and the World Bank are helping many states : Andhra Pradesh Water, Health, Sanitation Programme, India, Second Tamil Nadu Urban Development Project, Bangladesh Municipal Services Project, Arsenic Mitigation Water Supply Project are some of the examples that I got in very recent World Bank Report.

2. Bureaucracy and Management–Centralised Administration, lack of accountability, absence of elections in municipalities are dangerous elements. I got a case of Narharkatiya Town Committee, where the order of even the Supreme Court was not implemented for 25 years by Assam officers for reasons best known to all of them. This was implemented as soon as I came to know of the Hon'ble Court Order, and its implication. There is immediate need for Municipal Service (State) like Tamil Nadu where officers are transferable all over the state. Training and improvement in salary and service conditions are must. Surplus staff and top heavy administration should be removed.

3. Political Will – Why no political will in Assam for mass education/awareness for a healthy eco-system? Why birth

registration and child immunization programmes are not taken up seriously by Municipalities – despite stress given by the UNICEF?

I did not find political will in many schemes prepared by me: some of these are – (i) a STRAND ROAD – like Marine Drive– from Guwahati to Refinery area via Kharghuli, (ii) a Road in place of the existing Rail line from Guwahati Station to Refinery area and to Jalukbari side (University), (iii) A Ropeway to North Guwahati via Umananda, (iv) UBSP Programmes of Government of India, (v) Naharkatiya Town Tax Case (TATA Tea's Tea garden involved).

Why Acts/Rules are not framed and amended to serve public causes? Why no Rules for WETKABD & Wasteland Management and Rain Water Harvesting even today?

Why not improve data collection system ? Why no training programme for disaster-related activities? Why not set up an Institution like ILGUS of West Bengal for improving management skill ? Why not have regular state-level meetings for officers of all Municipalities/Town Committees?

A combination of measures will be needed with an action calendar as done by C.B. Naidu, CM of A.P. who had laid great emphasis on IDSMT programmes. The Central Government had already started lots of programmes like UBSP, EIUS, IDSMT, HUDCO programmes, Megacities Project, IUPEP etc. Have we shown our Political Will like C.B. Naidu of A.P.? In the Urban Initiatives India has focused on various themes such as : 1st Plan– refugee settlement and housing, 2nd Plan – land acquisition and development, 3rd Plan – Master plans/capitals, 4th Plan– land policy and finance, 5th Plan– urban poverty, 6th Plan– small and medium towns development, 7th Plan – urban basic services in backward towns, 8th Plan – strengthening urban local bodies, basic services and employment etc. How much have we done in Assam as per such focus?

Urban Master Planning is in crisis today. And Governments are not solving problems – they are only rearranging them. Let us learn from crisis. If the Government has the will – flood water can be changed in to drinking water. We have the ability. Let us apply our mind and compel the Poiticians to do the right thing at right moment.

10

EMPIRICAL EVIDENCE OF TRANSPORT PROBLEMS IN GAUHATI CITY

K.Bez

Introduction

The nature of transportation problem in an urban area is similar to any other urban areas, the magnitude however might differ. The commonest feature of urban transportation in most of the Indian cities is reflected by

(1) Either inadequacy or inefficiency of public means of transportation which as a result encourages the
(2) Growth of private means of transportation leading to increase in opportunity cost. With little or no chance to reduce because of physical or financial constraint for providing extra road length and improving the existing ones.

In general, road transportation is getting more importance than rail transport since 60% of goods traffic and 80% of passengers are carried by roads. Also, study revealed that traffic by road is expected to increase 10 to 12 p.c.p.a. (Padam, 1997, Gopalswami, 1997). This is also evident from data of Ministry of Surface Transport.

Year	(in billion Pass-Km)		(in billion ton-km)	
	Road	Rail	Road	Rail
1985	920	230	240	170
1995	3000	330	700	290
2000	5000	440	1500	360

In the urban areas road congestion happens to be a serious problem unless the number of vehicles with low carrying capacities are reduced. To do this, the efficiency of STUs needs to be improved also the size of fleet to be substantially increased.

Sometimes we blame the STUs for their failures but a very few of us did an indepth study to analyse the problems faced by the STUs. As much as 89 p.c. of its revenue earned spent on operation, we only see inefficiency and corruption. In a report of Transport Research Wing of the Ministry of Surface Transport, the financial viability of 71 State Road Transport Undertaking was given. It was observed that the financial viability of STUs is threatened by rising cost of operations, uneconomic fares, plying services on obligatory uneconomic routes, high level of taxation and strong competitor from the private operators.

The main problems of STUs are (a) poor financial performance, (b) inadequate infra-structures, (c) absence of rational fare policy, (d) high incidence of motor vehicle taxes, (e) large scale clandestine operations. All these contribute to inadequacy and inefficiency of public means of passenger transportation.

What do we gain by going private ?

- Congestion
- Environmental damage
- Declining use of public transport.

Yet there is no possibility to check the growth of car and 2-wheelers by providing attractive consumer friendly services by the STUs in near future. To me it appears that for the greater public interest not only we should integrate private operators with STUs but also needed active co-operation of car and 2-wheeler owners. The growth of cars, 2-wheelers and buses can be indicative of shift to private means of transportation in India, a decadal change could be observed:

Year	No. of vehicles/lakh		Population
	2–Wheelers	Car/Jeep	Bus
1971	1.05	1.24	0.17
1981	3.84	1.63	0.22
1990	12.32	2.45	0.35

In the city areas the trend is increasing. In a study of 12 metropolitan cities of India accounting 26% of total population showed that they have 60 to 70 p.c. of 2-wheelers and 13 p.c. of cars in the country, (Patankar 1989) and the metropolitan vehicle population has almost tripled since 1990 of which 65 p.c.vehicles are 2-wheelers. The vehicle density per km. of road varies from 98 in Madras to 838 (the highest) in Calcutta in term of passenger car unit.

The amount of pollution per bus-passenger-km and car or 2-wheeler pass-km when compared, there is a strong case for using the public means of transportation.

Gauhati Transport Situation

In studying urban transportation we need reliable data, this could be possible when survey is carried out by the investigator. Most important frame for planning transportation is consisted of

(1) Reliable data on incoming and out-going traffic.
(2) Demand for transportation as a zonal basis.
(3) Exact knowledge of car and other fast moving vehicles, their growth trend and the frequency of use.
(4) Purpose of trips made by passengers.
(5) Distribution of economic distances from the zones to the CBD.
(6) Daily influx of non-residential passengers.
(7) Transit passengers of rail, air also those road passengers whose end destination elsewhere.
(8) The volume of low moving means of transportation.

We are not fully satisfied with the reliability of data on Gauhati City Traffic and transportation. There is absolutely no data on passengers, passenger-km, the data on private modes of transportation and nearly no data on manual rickshaws and thelas including carts. We could imagine that being the centrally most important city of the North East, buses from other neighbouring states, city buses from other important townships also operating to and from Gauhati City. We need to make a thorough survey to analyse the demand for transportation, problems of transport and the problems arising out of transportation like pollution.

We spent many days shuttling from office to office for the governmental publications and other relevant information, we get some but there is a marked difference, *e.g.*

Year	Vehicles on Road			
	Bus	Car	2–wheelers	Auto
1993	1905	10,701	43,156	2845
1994	2061	12,130	50,800	3069
1995	1349	13,593	54,859	3193

Source : Transp. Statistics, Assam, 1997.

While the Town Planning Organisation which authored Gauhati Master Plan published in 1987 gave the number of buses as 1600 in 1979 and no information further. In a recent news item, it is said that 1500 buses are plying through Gauhati City Daily. We found from our own investigation that under each organisation the number of buses plying as follows:

Organisation	No. of buses
GGUMTA	500
GGMBOA	130
ASTC	71
OMNI	1000
Total	1701

Of which 1441 are operational. Besides there are daily services by private operators originated from other transport districts, but we do not have information on them.

Coming to car population we found that in Gauhati Master Plan, the actual data was given only for the year 1979. Their projected data for cars in 1991 is 31,428 which as nearly 3 times more the actual car population data of 1993. This is another drawback of car data.

Next the data on Motor Cycles and Scooters as reported in the Gauhati Master Plan :

Year	No. of motor-cycles/scooters
1979	7506
1991	90,723 (estimated)

The estimate of 1991 is more than double the numbers in 1993. We admit that break down of certain assumption may result in wrong estimation but this much wrong could not be tolerated.

Then we come to the other mode of private transportation– the Autos. Here, in this case no projection is made, the number of Auto in 1979 was 975, presently in 1999 this rose to 1794. The number of rickshaws in Gauhati city is 16,000 but more than double this number are unlicensed rickshaws in operation.

If we go by the projection of Town Planning department, the projected vehicle population of Gauhati in 1991 would be 304, 848, we do not have the breakdown data of vehicles except for cars, motor-cycles, therefore, we cannot truly think of vehicle density in terms of passenger-car units. Yet we may estimate somehow the vehicle density roughly. About 2000 trucks entered the city daily and 1400 buses that together makes 14,200 PCUs. There is 800 kms. of road length of which more than half is katcha, so not all of the length suitable for all vehicles. Even ignoring his fact the vehicles per km. of road is 381. This figure would increase when we would find the exact number of PCUs, yet probably would not be as bad as the metropolitan cities.

Demand for Passenger Transportation

We have made some estimation of demand, no sophisticated statistical tool is used for lack of data. Whatever data we got from the operating bus organisation, we make use of this. We got data on passengers carried in August month, 1998.

Daily passengers carried by different operators

Operators	No. of buses	Passengers	Pass-Km (estd.)
ASTC	46	32,548	423,124
GGUMTA	325	228,800	20,02,000
GGMBOA	70	49,480	544,280
OMNI BUS	1000	28,000	308,000

Other Modes

Type	No.	Pass	Pass -Km
Motor-cycle	75943	75,943	835,373
Cars	18085	36,170	397,870
Autos	2400	4,800	24,000

In estimating pass-km we take a few and point distances like Refinery, Engineering College, Gauhati University and Khanapara, which varies between 9 km and 13 km, we took simple average i.e.11 km. In case of Autos we took 4 km. as the trip length. In case of OMNI bus we think it is an intercity means of travel, since we are thinking of Gauhati City transport problem here also we might take as well 1 km as within city trip length.

We may now say that 102,843 PCUs carried 455,741 passengers per day in August 1998. We can estimate for other months and years provided we get the set of independent variables. Now we try to see how the congestion problem be minimized by transferring all the passengers from the low capacity vehicles to buses.

If we transfer all the passengers of cars i.e. 36170 persons to bus with seat capacity 45 with the same norm of 16 trips (8 round trips) per bus then we need 50 additional buses.

Similarly, when motor-cycle and scooter borne passengers are transferred to bus, we need another fleet of 105 bases. At the same time the reduction of vehicle density/km of road would be 93,563 PCUs/day (= 75943 + 18085—155 x 3).

With the usual or existing modes to vehicle density km. of road in Gauhati happended to be 126 PCUs/km. If the transfer from cars and motor-cycle is probable then the vehicles density would be 9 PCUs/km of road. This, of course, does not mean that it will be that much of reduction in congestion. Because, we take that the services of rickshaws and Autos are atleast indispensable. We did not take into account other slow moving means of transport like thelas, carts also the trucks operating within and through the city. Let us not forget the bi-cycles.

Some survey was carried out by town and country planning organisation in 13 different localities of the city to study congestion and the necessary steps to be taken for improvement. One interesting point in this study revealed that the slow moving traffic volume consisted of 15 p.c. to 61 p.c. of the total volume of traffic in P.C.Us. This confirms the requirement for mass transport facilities in some pockets urgently. Probably the survey was done sometimes before 1987, the situation might have improved or be worse as the demand for transport increase at the rate of about 10 p.c. annually. Also, it was not reported time interval, time period of the peak hours, but by judging the total traffic volume from a minimum 1785 PCUs to a maximum of 23475 PCUs, the time interval must be one hour or more.

We know that like in other big cities the low capacity vehicles accounts for 96 p.c. of the total, the public means of transport i.e. buses contributes only 4 p.c. and the private modes of transportation is as high 93 p.c. Although, we admit that there is some doubt regarding the reliability of data, nevertheless the rapid increase of private means of transportation stays confirmed. This is the principal cause of congestion. Also the cars and motor cycles contribute more to pollution. A bus carrying 45 passengers runs 1 km/3.5 litre to 4 litres of diesel and a motor cycle would accomplish 25 pass-km per litre of petrol. The shift to public means of transportation means :

(1) to halt declining trend of speed
(2) to reduce road congestion
(3) to save energy.

According to National Transport Policy Committee energy consumption by car .025 litre/pass-km and by bus .0048 litre/pass-km. Therefore, there is a strong case for modal shift from private to public modes of transportation. We think that prohibitive road tax and charge for parking facilities, congestion, air pollution are not sufficient deterrence for dissuading to use private modes of transportation, but I suggested once in a seminar organised by N.E. Indian Town Planner Organisation that a quota system be introduced in rationing scarce road space and spares congestion.

Concluding Remark

Excluding the pedestrians, the cyclists, passengers arriving by rail, air and water, the volume of passengers by other modes is nearly 5 lakhs per day in Gauhati, which roughly 0.5 trips per person per day. This related to 1998. We may add another 10 p.c. this year. The volume of transport vehicles motorised or manual including 7025 trucks and 10,000 thelas barring the information on bicycles and carts, we have nearly 137,968 P.C.Us. in Gauhati, which speaks for extra road space.

The problem of Gauhati City transport could be felt but we really know very little what particular aspects of city transports be improved without disrupting the seemingly co-herence with different class of operators or tilting the balance between operation and infrastructures. I certainly feel that there is a case for investigation.

Recently there are articles with vitriolic remarks about the functioning of ASTC but none has touched the root cause of financial crisis, corruption along is thought to be omnipotent devil. In case of STU, the government is master but not performing as such. Say many accuses that ASTC employees 10 persons per bus, many of the efficient STUs do almost employ the same. Some clandestine operations are made but that cannot make STUs inefficient. When government wanted to do the social service for them by the STUs, the government should also prepare to compensate. I do not mind privatisation but I dare say Indians are not ethical, the private masters would not distinguish between a basket of chicken and passengers. People who talk about running profitably by private operators–do they know anything about social and moral responsibility of private operators? The private operators have scant regard for passenger amenities or comfort.

References

Bez, K.; Pollution by Transportation, specially in urban Areas, paper presented to N.E.I.Town Planning Org. seminar, 1998.

Demand for Transportation, Netherland School of Economics, Rotterdam, 1976.

Fouracrae, P.R.: A comparison of Public Transport in the 3 Medium sized cities, CIRT, 1986.

Padam, S. to 21st Century by bus in *Ind. Jour. Transp. Manag.* Vol.21, No.4, 1997.

Patankar, P.G. : *Urban Transport in Distress*, CIRT, 1989.

Satyaramchander, A.; Vehicular Polluition in Urban Areas in *Ind. Town Trans. Manag.*, Feb, 1997.

Sen, S.: *Demand for Transportation*, Ph. D.Thesis, NEHU, 1994.

11

PROBLEMS OF ROAD TRANSPORT IN GUWAHATI CITY SINCE 1972

C. Sharma & N. Bhattacharyya

Introduction

Guwahati, the gateway of North-eastern Region is not only the capital of Assam but could be said as the economic capital of the seven states including Meghalaya, Manipur, Nagaland, Tripura, Mizoram and Arunachal Pradesh mainly because of its geographical location (Fig. 11.1). The city has tremendous importance in economic, social, education, commercial and transport activities in the region.

The tiny settlement of Guwahati in the Ahom era assumed the status of administrative headquarters during the British period. After independence, particularly after shifting of capital of Assam from Shillong to Dispur (Guwahati) in 1972, the city grew rapidly for which the overall environment deteriorated at very fast rate. Occupying an unique location at the bank of the mighty river Brahmaputra, the city possess beautiful hills and hillocks, river islands and sandy chars. However, in the recent years all these beautiful features have been degraded and the city as a whole polluted in such a way that the life become so miserable for the

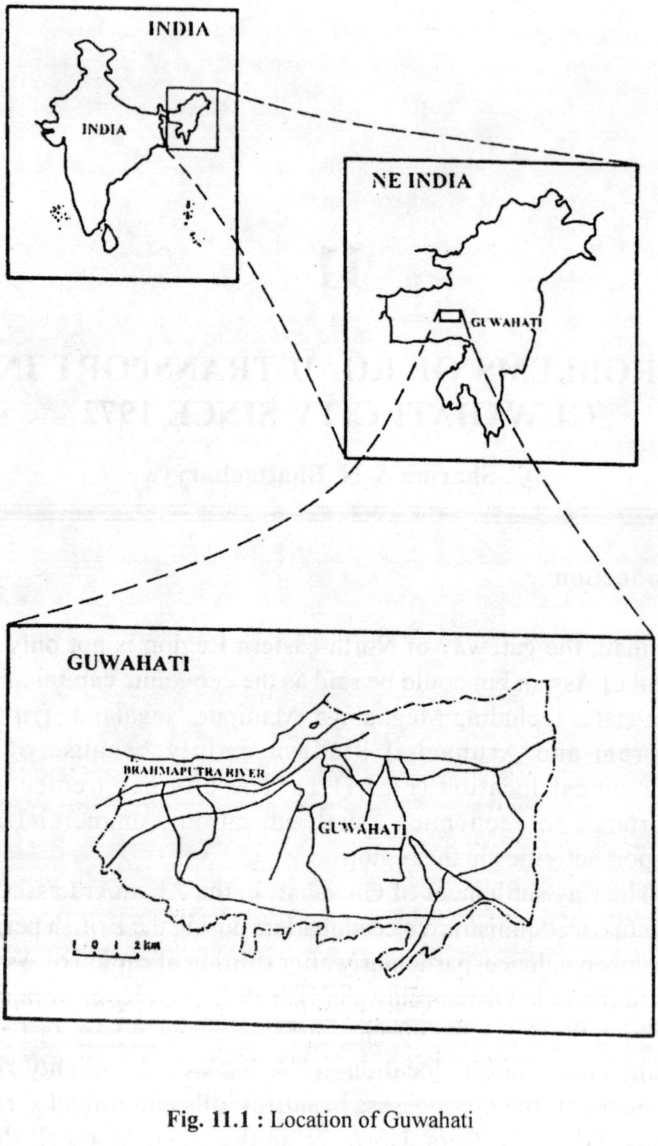

Fig. 11.1 : Location of Guwahati

city dwellsers. Haphazard growth of built up areas, unplanned landuse, roadside garbage made the city look an ugly one.

The present study aims at discussing some of the issues related to transport and associated problems. Increase of all types of vehicles and disproportionate growth of other amenities and road space cause deterioration of city environement (Fig.11.2). Almost all the remedial measures taken by the concern departments so far are adhoc in nature. Proper planning for traffic management and for other amenities has not been done so far. Even the necessary data for efficient planning are not yet made available. Here, in this study, an attempt has been made to generate a data base for traffic management and in solving associated problems.

Methodology

The present study has been taken up with the objective of understanding the transport pattern and the problems of traffic with this. The study has mainly done based on the data generated directly from the field. In regard to various category of transport means data have been collected from District Transport and Municipal Corporation Offices. To know about the traffic flow and congestion points along with hourly variation a few points have been selected for minitoring. Categorywise traffic pressure on various roads have been measured by direct observation. The information related to parking, pollution etc. have incorporated here from various reports and published documents. Some of the collected data have been presented with tables and figures using suitable statistical methods.

Analysis and Findings

The problem of transportation in Guwahati has been studied from four different angles as it was tried by Robinson and Bawford in case of European cities. These are :

(i) Trip generation
(ii) Trip distribution
(iii) Network description
(iv) Traffic management and model development.

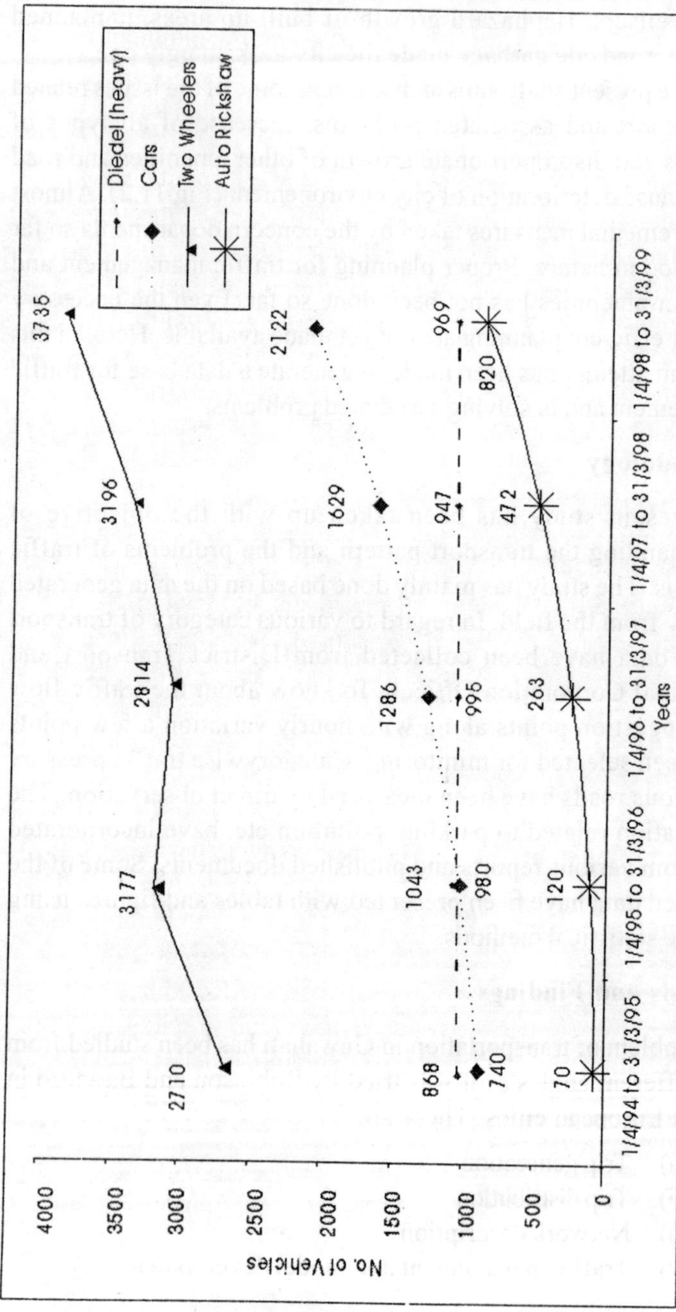

Fig. 11.2 : Trend of Registered Vehicles in Guwahati (1994 to 1999)

Trip Generation

In trip generation it has been tried to describe the reasons why trips are made and how it is generated. In case of Guwahati trip generation of all sorts of vehicle depend on :

(a) Opportunity provided by the city.
(b) Locational advantage of the city.
(c) Demand for specialised goods and services offered by the city.
(d) Available facilities in neighbouring towns.
(e) Administrative pull.

As the city is located at the most accessible point from all the urban centres of entire north eastern states the pressure of population increase day by day and as a result more functions added to the city. Most of the specialised facilities, i.e. goods and services concentrated in Guwahati. On the other hand more people use to come from neighbouring towns and villages to Guwahati to avail such opportunities. Over and above administrative pull is the main cause of population growth and concentration of specialised activities. It has been reflected in the growth of population after shifting of capital from Shillong in 1972 (Fig. 11.3).

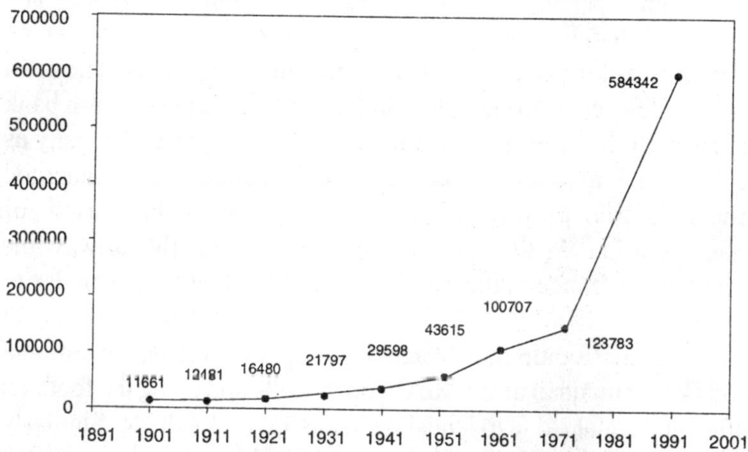

Fig 11.3 : Population - Guwahati City

Trip Distribution

In trip distribution the number of trips between different zones have been measured. As many as 24 city bus routes are there in Guwahati. The flow of buses and other traffic on all these routes are increasing though not uniform throughout (Table 11.1 & 11.2). There is significant difference in number of vehicles on road in up and down journey. Significant variation also observed in various days of the week.

Hourly variation is found to be more important which is mainly responsible for causing traffic congestion in many areas. City dwellers now facing a serious problem of traffic congestion particularly at school and office going hours. Similar is the situation in the afternoon hours i.e. at the return time. The worst affected areas have been identified here are, Guwahati club, Silpukhuri, Chandmari, Ulubari, Ganeshguri, Bhangagarh, Paltanbazar and Fancybazar.

Travel Description

The travel description here in Guwahati includes road type and road condition, network description, travel distance, travel cost, travel time, traffic capacity and travellers choice and behaviour.

Guwahati has total geographical area of 217 sq. km. of which almost two-third covered either by hills or by wetlands. The main railway line, connecting upper and lower Assam in the south bank of river Brahmaputra divided the city into two parts. As many as 109.34 sq. km. of land in the city used for residential, commercial and industrial purposes, while 9.71 sq. km. of land used for transportation. As the hills and wetlands and also the railway line stand as hindrance in the road network the travel time increase to a great extent. Railway line is responsible for traffic congestion in the places like Santipur, Athgaon, Kumarpara, Paltanbazar, Sarania and Bamunimaidan areas. Roads on the hills and along the foothills often get damage due to landslide, landslip, rock fall etc. Similarly the roads along or across the wetlands and low-lying areas often get damage due to excessive moisture and inundation during the rainy months. Road capacity in terms of its width is very less compared to traffic load. In both new and old residential areas car driving is extremely difficult for the narrowness of roads supplemented by roadside parking, garbages and violation of traffic rules. Travellers choice is mainly depends on cost and time factors rather than comfort. For example, those who can spend more in travelling choose either autorickshaw or express buses. Again the office going people particularly the women and the guardians who have the responsibility to take their children to school usually opt express buses to manage time. The use of slow moving vehicles like rickshaws belong to congested residential areas. Bitter relationship between passengers and bus conductors or rickshaw pullers often observed in the city. The conflicts normally arise mainly at the time of collecting fairs. Overcrowding in the buses and asking for exorbitant fair by rickshaw pullers are the two important causes for such situation.

Table 11.1 : Hourly variation of traffic in selected routes of Guwahati

Type of Vehicle	Time								
	5am to 7 am			7 am to 9 am			9 am to 11am		
	Route1	Route2	Route 3	Route1	Route 2	Route 3	Route1	Route 2	Route 3
Car/Jeep/Van	115	127	66	401	475	188	681	924	445
Autorickshaw	32	78	46	82	262	151	184	424	219
Scooter/M-Cycle	80	83	70	297	544	254	460	752	479
Bus/Truck	109	175	120	170	289	270	221	371	234
Other motorised	7	38	8	7	60	7	36	66	31
Rickshaw	46	90	84	70	155	180	160	57	230
Bicycle	86	165	154	223	500	192	289	368	223
Other non-motorised	8	29	30	11	55	43	39	34	62

Route – 1 – R.G. Barua Road (Near Zoo)
Route – 2 – G.S. Road (Bhangagarh)
Route – 3 – G.N.B. Road (Silpukhuri)

Table 11.2 : Variation of city bus frequency in different routes

Route	Frequency of Buses	Trip Interval (In minute)
• Basistha - Garpandu via Chandmari	> 100	< 5
• Churchfield - Khanapara via Paltanbazar		
• Kahilipara - Garpandu via Chandmari	50 - 100	10 - 12
• Hengerabari - Garpandu via G.S. Rd.		
• Hatigaon - Garpandu via Chandmari	30 - 50	15 - 25
• Jorabat - Garpandu via Narengi		
• Forestgate - Chandrapur via Panikhaiti		
• Ayurvedic College - Panjabari via Chandmari		
• Pandu - Patharquarry		
• Churchfield - Chaygaon		
• Forestgate - Garpandu via Uzanbazar	20 - 30	20 - 30
• Garchuk - Churchfield via Fatashil Ambari		
• VIP - Medical College via Paltanbazar		
• Churchfield - Majhirgaon via Maligaon		
• G.M.C. - Sualkuchi via Kachari		
• Others routes (10 Nos. of Private City Bus routes)	< 20	25 - 35

Traffic Management and Model Development

For the proper management of traffic and for forecasting travel dimensions transportation models have to develop. For this, model split i.e. the phasing of activities is necessary. Unlike the three other approaches the positioning of model split is neither fixed nor regularly definable since elements are part of the systems which have relations with transport development. For forecasting, important variables like population, employment, personal income and expenditure are often considered. Here in Guwahati, population concentration in respect of available space for settlement, is very high. As a result newer settlements have pushed either towards the hills or towards the wetlands. As such the transport management in the city become difficult and single model for it is not enough. The development in all transport means, the proportion between private and public vehicles, road space and number of vehicles, population growth and transport network expansion are fast changing in Guwahati. As such no single model could be suggested for transport planning in Guwahati. However, a general consensus may be evolved for development of transportation in Guwahati if the trend of development in each factor monitored and merged together qualitatively and quantitatively.

Conclusion

As the city of Guwahati facing various traffic problems which are increasing day by day, the remedial measures have to be taken up without delay. For this, an attempt has to be made by all concern departments collectively. To get proper directions and planning to take necessary action an acceptable model has to be evolved considering the present situation and the trend of changes at least in last few years. To do so a strong data base is required which is not yet generated at any level. In this paper an attempt has been made to pinpoint certain facts based on data generated directly from the field. Though it is only a part of whole planning process of efficient transport management in Guwahati, this study may help in understanding the vital transport related issues in the city.

References

Alam, Shah Maznoor, 1965 : *Hyderabad-Secunderabad (Twin cities). A study in Urban Geography*, Allied Pub. Pvt. Ltd., Bombay.

Bhattacharyya, N.N., 1998 : *Morphology of the Towns of Assam with Special Reference to the City of Guwahati. (Analytico-synthetic study) Guwahati.*

Carter, Harold, 1977 : *The Study of Urban Geography*. Edward Arnold, London.

Dutta, A.K., 1964 : An analysis of Communication to the Metropolis of Calcutta, *National Geographical Journal of India*, Vol. X, Part 3 & 4

Kumar Naresh, 1991 : *Geography of Transportation : Commodity Flows and Human Interaction in Meerut City*, Concept Pub., New Delhi, pp. 7-38.

Panday, N.P., 1990 : *Geography of Transport*, Inter-India Pub. pp 73-136.

Robinson and Bawford, C.B., 1978 : 'Transportation Planning'. *Geography of Transport*, Mcdonald & Evans, pp 383-97

Sharma, C., 1988 : *City Bus Service in the City of Guwahati : A Geographical Study*. M. Phil Dissertation (Unpublished), Gauhati University.

12

GUWAHATI CITY : Problems and Some Likely Solutions

A. K. Afsar Hazarika & Amiyo Kr. Sharma

Guwahati city, popularly called "the gateway to the North-East" does not give a very good impression to the newcomer when he enters the city. The first impression is that of a chaotic situation arising out of totally mismanaged traffic and haphazard growth of shops and commercial establishment with total disregard to cleanliness, discipline and other qualities of civilised life.

The scenario was much different during the sixties and early seventies i.e. prior to the shifting of the capital from Shillong when the population was within manageable limits and the civic services could reach its citizens. Over the last decade and half things have gone from bad to worse. Due to financial constraints and to a great extent faulty planning and adhocism in execution of various schemes by the Government and other civic authorities have turned this once beautiful city into a veritable garbage heap which is now gasping for breath without any sign of improvement in the near future.

Against this backdrop, there have been attempts from some conscientious citizens, activist groups, town planners from time to time to formulate some sort of an action plan for the Government to work on, but due to lack of sustained pressure, the efforts did not bear fruit.

Let us make an attempt to first identify the problem areas broadly and seek solutions one by one.

Waterlogging

The worst affected areas are G.N.B. Road, R.G. Baruah Road and eastern part of G.S.Road, Santipur, Bharalumukh etc. The encroachment on the hills from Nabagraha upto Noonmati and indiscriminate earthcutting resorted to by the encroachers have resulted in heavy silting of the drainage system making it totally incapable of taking care of the heavy discharge during the monsoon months. Besides, with the increase in population over the years, the storm water reservoirs like Sola Beel, Deepor Beel and drainage like Bahini, Khanajan etc. along with several low-lying and marshy areas are getting reduced everyday due to siltation, encroachment and earthfilling for building construction as a result of which the rain water takes a long time to drain out.

To reduce/prevent waterlogging some short and long term measures need to be taken immediately:

- To initiate soil protection measures all along the hilltops/slopes from Nabagraha hills upto Noonmati hills by large scale plantation of trees, turfing etc. with technical expertise from landscapers/planners and concerned departments. At the same time, efforts should be made to evict the encroachers, if possible otherwise motivate them to initiate soil protection measures locally, failing which punitive action should be taken against the violators.
- Construction of side drains with silt traps all along the foothills from Nabagraha upto Noonmati so that the silt gets deposited into the traps and only the water drains out. Steps should be taken to clear the silt regularly during the monsoon period. This work should be started on a priority basis immediately, if necessary on a selected portion before the onset of monsoon this year as an experiment. Local people should be involved during the execution so that quality of the work is monitored by the residents who suffer the most due to waterlogging.

- Once the aforesaid work is commenced, steps should be taken to clear/repair the underground drains/footpaths along the G.N.B. Road.
- All encroachments on both sides of the Bahini river should be removed and excavation of the bed resorted to on a priority basis before the monsoon, to increase carrying capacity of the rivers.
- Necessary penal provisions should be initiated for throwing garbage into the drains by the residents and commercial establishments in the entire city and proper punishment should be meted out to the violators as an exemplary measure so that it acts as a deterrent.

Traffic Congestion

The traffic congestion has become a common problem for the citizens of the city and every passing day, the situation is becoming bad to worse. Unless some serious thought is not given immediately, a day will come when there will be no movement on some of the major roads like G.N.B. Road for hours together. The stretch of G.N.B. Road starting from Guwahati Club upto Chandmari flyover is the worst affected one.

Before we go into the details, it would perhaps be necessary to deal briefly on the origin of the problem. Till the sixties or early seventies the roads all over the city appeared to be wide enough to cater to the needs of the existing traffic at that time. But with the gradual growth of vehicular population during the last two decades, the roads could not keep up. The most common remedy like widening is not possible because there is not adequate 'roadside reserve'. Government land and acquisition of the periodic patta land from the landholders is prohibitively expensive. Unless external funding is made available and legal bottlenecks are removed, it would not be possible to widen the existing road in the foreseeable future. As a temporary solution following steps may be initiated.

- Impose ban on the movement of slow moving vehicles initially hand cart and pony cart along the G.N.B. Road from Guwahati Club upto Bamunimaidam during the period from 7 a.m. to 8 p.m.

on all days except Sunday. Allow plying of rickshaws until such time the Auto rickshaws are disciplined. Guwahati is probably only city in the country where auto-rickshaws do not ply by the metre and no action is taken as per the appropriate sections of relevant Act. It is expected that once the autorickshaws start plying by the meter, Government could go for removing the rickshaws initially from the major roads and eventually from the entire city.

- One of the other major factors responsible for traffic snarl ups is the City Bus. The old and rickety city buses do not follow any traffic rule and runs by the whims and fancies of the driver. Further, Guwahati city has too many stoppages (some even at a distance of 100-200 mtr from one another) compared to the distances of 1 ½ to 2 km in other parts of the country. This needs to be done immediately. In this connection it may be pointed out that the District Administration of Kamrup had initiated bold steps to remove altogether 61 stoppages along different routes in the city but could not implement fully because of resistance from a section of the public who wants to avail the bus service to and from their doorstep.
- Almost all the city bus stoppages are opposite to each other for up and down traffic thereby restricting the road width and causing traffic congestion. This needs to be rectified and care should be taken so as to remove all such stoppages at the road intersections, which adds to the traffic congestion.
- Improved road lighting will go a long way in making our streets safe for driving. All the street lights should be shifted from the sides to the 'central verge'. Efforts in this regard seems to have been made in case of a portion of G.S. Road which is very much welcome.
- Guwahati Traffic Police should make it mandatory for all drivers to use dippers while driving in the night within the city. The harsh glare of the headlights have caused innumerable fatal accidents especially along the G.S. Road in the past.
- All traffic points should be installed with electronic traffic lighting systems and manual regulation should be stopped.

Necessary financial resources for this could be mobilised through commercial organisation dealing in tyres, lubricants etc.

- One of the major cause of traffic congestion along the A.T./ G.S.Road in the city is the plying of tourist buses to and from the other six N.E. States numbering a few hundred every day and night. There should be an Inter-State Bus Terminus (ISBT) preferably along Jalukbari-Khanapara NH way somewhere near Pub Boragaon, where required government land should be available. In fact, the District Administration had initiated such a project way back in 1993-94 but subsequently it was not followed up.
- Public transportation system should be improved and public should be encouraged to use public transport as much as possible.
- Metered Local Taxi should be introduced.
- Local train services should be introduced between Kamakhya and Narengi at an interval of every 30 mts. during peak hours.
- City Traffic Police should be vested with power to impose fine and other penal provisions on the spot.
- One of the major causes of traffic congestion in the city is VIP/VVIP movement on the main roads.
- Footpaths should be maintained properly and all encroachments should be removed so that the pedestrians are not compelled to walk on the road instead of the footpaths. Overhead pedestrian crossings should be constructed in busy intersections like Ulubari, Ganeshguri, Maligaon Chariali, DC's Court, Guwahati Club, Chandmari etc.
- There should be separate road for slow-moving traffic. One possibility may be to approach the railway authority to allow 'right of use' of about six metres of land on both sides of the railway tracks right from Jalukbari to Narengi, which could be converted into a road exclusively for slow moving traffic. Such a proposal was also mooted by the District Administration during 1993-94 but subsequently was not followed up.
- The city of Guwahati has seen mushrooming growth of private

schools over the last few years and the situation now has become so acute that during school hours the traffic condition in almost the whole city goes crazy. It is not understood how and why the regulatory authorities issue permission to such schools with total disregard to public inconvenience. Government should direct the concerned authorities to examine all pros and cons before acceding to such proposals which is detrimental to public interest.

- Government should designate specific places for parking of vehicles, so that 'NO PARKING' violations could be dealt with firmly by the traffic police. Time has come to think of construction of multi-storied car parking complex by private participation. If necessary, finance at concessional rate of interest should be made available from financial institutions to private entrepreneurs/ corporate bodies under profit-sharing agreement.
- All kinds of garages, workshops and commercial establishments are seen to be functioning on both sides of the city roads and a major portion of the road reserved land is being encroached upon by these establishments adding to the traffic congestion. These need to be removed and firm penal action should be initiated under appropriate sections of law.
- The Khanapara-Jorabat portion of the NH way is the alone entry and exit point for the vehicular traffic to and from the five NE states. Considering the huge volume of traffic the present width of the road is totally inadequate which very often leads to traffic congestion lasting several hours. This vital portion of the NH may be taken up for widening to six lanes and the work could be taken up under 'Build Own Operate Transfer' (BOOT) basis through private participation within a fixed time frame.

Maintenance of Parks and Open Spaces

Guwahati has probably one of the least number of parks and open spaces for its citizens and whatever few exists the maintenance is very poor. Considering the acute financial crisis facing the civil bodies like the Guwahati Municipal Corporation, all such parks should be handed over to private corporate houses for beautification and maintenance so that its own resources are deployed for other priority projects.

Senior citizens of Guwahati often talk about the vast open space they enjoyed right from the present Latasil field up to the GMC Water works a part of which was a polo ground meant for the then rulers. While appreciating the need for more and more land for development during the post-independence period has led to disappearance of this vast open space and but for only the small Latasil field as it exists today the Judges' Field is hardly available for its citizen's use since the same is almost continuously remains under occupation of the District Administration for Government's use. Now since, Government has declared the site for permanent capital for the state behind Hengerabari area, efforts should be made to hold all Government functions/meetings/demonstrations etc. in a suitable field somewhere near the capital site and make arrangements for releasing the Judges' field for the benefit of citizens of Guwahati. Recently, the Deputy Commissioner, Kamrup is seen to have taken some initiative in this regard which is welcome.

As mentioned earlier, the earthcutting within the Guwahati city by some unscrupulous persons has caused heavy silting of drainage and dust pollution in the city. As an additional measure for environmental protection, schemes, like 'city forest' and 'smriti van' may be introduced. There are quite a few vacant Government plots available within the city which could be used for the purpose. More and more public participation is required for success of major plantation or environment protection/preservation schemes. Social Forestry, Soil Conservation and such other departments should be directed to carry out awareness campaigns amongst the worst affected population in the hill slopes and local residents should be involved in all such schemes.

And last but the most important factor in any development effort is the involvement of its citizens. Unless they are convinced and motivated towards making their own city worth living in, no amount of efforts from either Government or any private organisation will bear fruit. There should be public pressure groups actively involved in the decision making process in selection of schemes and they should strengthen the hands of the Government in giving concrete shape to all such projects within their locality. However, this does not mean that they will oppose each and every move from the Government just for the sake of opposition.

13

SOME NATURAL AND MAN-MADE ENVIRONMENTAL PROBLEMS OF GUWAHATI

S.K. Sarmah & Dattabarua

Introduction

Guwahati is the premier city of north-east India and is the centre of commerce, education and other cultural activities. Historically, the old city of Pragjyotishpur is thought to be located in or nearabout Guwahati. But unlike many other ancient cities of India, very few ancient historical ruins are found in and around Guwahati. During Ahome rules, it was a fortified city with ramparts (garhs) to prevent the advancement of Moghuls to the east.

The British rulers did not consider it fit to be the capital of the state of Assam, mainly due to unhygienic and bad climatic conditions of the city, and established the capital in Shillong, more than 100 km south of Guwahati, at Khasi and Jayantia hills. When the state of Meghalaya was carved out of Assam, the capital of truncated Assam had to be brought down to Guwahati in a hurry in 1972. This resulted in haphazard growth and population explosion in the city, giving rise to environmental problems.

Physiography

Guwahati is a city of hills and marshy land. Hills surround the eastern, southern and western sides. The heights of these hills are less than 300 metres from the mean sea lavel. The hills are Chunsali, Chitrachal, Japorigog, Narakasur, Fatasil, Gotanagar, Nilachal and branches of Khasi and Jayantia hills. To the north, is the river Brahmaputra flowing from east to west. The shape of the city is just like a bowl with protrusions like Sarania Janardan hills having height less than 200 metres. Of the 216 sq. km. of the city area about 10 sq. km. area are under water bodies such as Deepor beel, Numali Jalah, Silsako beel, Ghorajan, Silagrant beel, Barsapara, Tilingaon beel, Paschim Boragaon and other smaller water bodies.

Population

The environmental degradation and pollution of an area is directly related to the number of people living in it. As per census report of 1876, the area of Guwahati was 6.74 sq. km. with a population of 11,492 the density being 1705 person per sq. km. When Guwahati Municipality was converted to Corporation, with an area of 216 sq. km., in 1974, its population was 2,53,851 the density of population being 1175 person per sq. km. The population projected by G.M.C. in an area of 216 sq. km. became 4,51,200 with population density of 2089 person per sq. km. in 1981. Again for the same area, population became 5,77,591 as per 1991 census, with a density of 2674 per sq. km. Thus the population became more than double within a period of 26 years from 1974 to 1991, within the same area. Land suitable for habitation and other developmental activities being highly limited, hills, wetlands, and other open spaces were encroached upon for different purposes by Government, private agencies and individuals, resulting in cutting down of hills, filling up of low-lying areas and deforestation. These activities have created environmental problems in the city.

Effect on climatological parameters

According to Assam Remote Sensing Application Centre, the land use for residential purposes was 64.6% in 1967-68, which increased to 73% of the total area in 1990. Densely populated areas are Athgaon, Fancy Bazar, Lakhtokia, Paltan Bazar, Ulubari areas, where high-rise buildings have formed concrete jungles. The result is the formation of heat islands in these areas and cold islands in other parts due to unequal heating of the surfaces. Formation of these islands give rise to erretic air circulation. Maximum temperature is found to be decreasing since about 1978 which may be due to increasing air pollution. Similarly minimum temperature is increasing from about the same time, indicating urbanisation.

There is diminishing trend of rainfall in the city since about 1970, which may be attributed to the deforestation of the city hills and urbanisation. Within the city, the highest rainfall occurs along a strip from Bharalumukh to Noonmati and Japorigog hills. Lowest rainfall occurs in the Kalapahar-Ulubari area.

High rainfall in the north-eastern and eastern hills is responsible for water logging in the Chandmari-Noonmati-R.G. Barooah Road area, as natural storm-water reservoirs have been filled up for settlement and other development activities. Besides, use of faulty rainfall data in designing drains, encroachment of Bharalu river, and drains chocked by silts from denuded hills, have given rise to these environmental problems.

Due to fomation of persistent heat islands in the Panbazar-Paltanbazar area and cold island in the Ulubari-Japorigog area, the wind-flow pattern in the city shows great variations. The flow pattern is governed mainly by orography but modified by built-up areas in the Fancybazar-Panbazar-Paltanbazar area giving rise to anticyclonic convergence. But wind flows towards the city from Brahmaputra throughout the year.

Air Pollution

The main contribution to air pollution comes from fossil-fuelled vehicles and industrial activities. According to a report from Traffic Police Department in 1998, the number of various kinds of vehicles plying in the city are : 3000 medium capcity, 4000 heavy duty, 28000 light, 8000 autorickshaws. These vehicles ply in about 806 km of the city roads. They emit pollutants like hydrocarbon, Carbon mono-oxide, sulphur-di-oxide, Nitrogen-di-oxide and fine hard particles (SPM). A motor vehicle covering a distance of 1 km will emit 2 gms of HC, 25 gms of CO, 1.8 gms of NO, 0.3 gms of particulate matters and 0.5 gms of SO_2. Depending on the types of vehicle, age and types of fuel used, there may be some variations in these values.

Although no figure is available for vehicles plying in the city in the earlier part of seventies, we can safely assume that it was much less compared to the present day figures.

Within the city, there are several industries such as oil refinery, asbestos factory, iron works, carbon related industry, leather industry, soap factory, chemical industry, biscuit factory and miscellaneous small scale industries. The number of industries are increasing day by day. These industries also contribute to the air, water and soil pollution in the city. Of all the pollutants, SPM has exceeded the tolerance limit of 200 microgrammes per cubic metre of air, in many parts of the city. However, the other pollutants such as oxides of nitrogen and sulphur, hydrocarbon, metallic dusts show values lower than the permissible levels.

Water Pollution

Because of increased population there is scarcity of drinking water in the city. Piped water from Guwahati Municipal Corporation and other, can serve only one-third of the population. So, most of the people depend on river or ground water. Due to excessive water drawn by the multi-storied ownership flats, the amount of ground water in the city is dwindling. The qualities of water from these non-conventional sources, greatly deviates from standards required for physical, inorganic and organic materials and bacteriological parameters, in drinking water.

The water of Bharalu river, along its entire length, was sparkling with aquatic flora and fauna before independence. But deterioration of its water quality started after independence due to increased population and industrialization. The stretch of the river from Zoo road to Bharalumukh became highly polluted after 1970, due to heavy concentration of population, discharge of some refinery wastes, effluents from small scale industries and garbages. Seven major drains carry waste products of the city, to the river. The water contains high amount of sulphide, ammonia, oil, low dissolve oxygen, high amount of BOD and COD, high amount of alkalinity, high turbidity and disagreeable odour.

Noise Pollution

Human ear can hear sound when the vibration lies between 20-20,000 Hz. But it became injurious to health when the vibrations exceed 250-10,000 Hz in frequency. A healthy man can tolerate intensity of sound upto 85 decibel level. Beyond that it is harmful to man. Various measurements by Assam Pollution Control Board have shown that sound intensity level has exceeded that limit, in the busy hours of the day, in Ganeshguri, Ulubari, Silpukhuri, Fancybazar, Adabari, Beltola, Chariali and Guwahati Club. Increasing number of vehicles, increase in population, and various kinds of human activities have been responsible for noise pollution.

Conclusions

Peculiar topography, population explosion and various human activities have influenced the climatological parameters, and increase in the level of air-water-noise pollution. Environmental problems have become more acute in the city after shifting of the capital from Shillong.

References

Dattabarua, P. (1992) : "A study of climatology and a few air quality parameters of Guwahati area". Gauhati University.

News letters published by Assam Pollution Control Board, Vol. IV (2), 1994: Vol. VIII (2,3,4), 1998.

Sarma, C. (1987) : "A study of some water quality parameters from different sources of water in Guwahati area". Gauhati University.

Sarmah, H.P. (1987) : "A study of some water quality parameters of Bharalu river at Guwahati". Gauhati University.

Sharms, S.K : *Assam Tribune* and *Dainik Asom* during the last ten years.

14

RETROGRADING ENVIRONMENT IN GUWAHATI
A Geographical Analysis

Pradip Sharma & Mahfuza Rahman

Introduction

The environmental degradation is not only problem of the developed countries but a global one which affect all the living beings on the surface of the earth. With the rapid increase of population and with fast changing economic activities, natural environment in India have deteriorated day by day. Guwahati being the only city of North-eastern region witnessed fast growth in many respects. Rapid growth of population, depletion of forest cover, spread of diseases have been common in this city which have resulted in a series of environmental problems akin to land, air, water and society. In the recent years specific localised problems have risen alarmingly threatening the very existence of a safe and healthy life of the citizens.

Guwahati has always been an important centre of intense economic, social, educational, commercial and transport activities. Rapid growth of population mainly due to rural urban migration, influx of labour from other states and also from neighbouring countries forced the city to expand its area extends haphazardly. This has resulted in overcrowding of settlement areas and encroachment on hill tops, hillslides and wetlands. In turn, this has led the city to bear the hazards of air, water, noise pollution along with the problems created due to waterlogging and waste disposal in Guwahati in the recent years. Multiple effect between population and pollution and the cause of various types of pollution in the city have been analysed (Figs. 14.1 and 14.2). Based on the findings, intervention points have been identified to curb various types of pollution in the city, and suggestions made.

Objectives

The main objectives of the study are :

(i) To highlight in changing scenario of Guwahati in respect of environmental quality after shifting of capital to Dispur;
(ii) To identify the most populated areas in the city;
(iii) To discuss the major causes of pollution;
(iv) To identify the intervention points for the solution of environmental problems in the city; and
(v) To suggest some of the measures for minimising pollution and improve overall environment of the city.

Database and Methodology

The study is based on data and information collected from both primary and secondary sources. With the monitoring equipments and technical help from Pollution Control Board, Assam, primary data have been generated. To measure the level of pollution particularly noise, vehicular emission and solid waste related aspects, monitoring points have been selected in the city. Waterlogging and associated environmental problems have been studied covering almost all the affected areas within the city. Information about the water quality and relevant data for measuring air pollution have been collected from Pollution Control Board, Assam Ground Water Board and the findings of various research works. The data thus

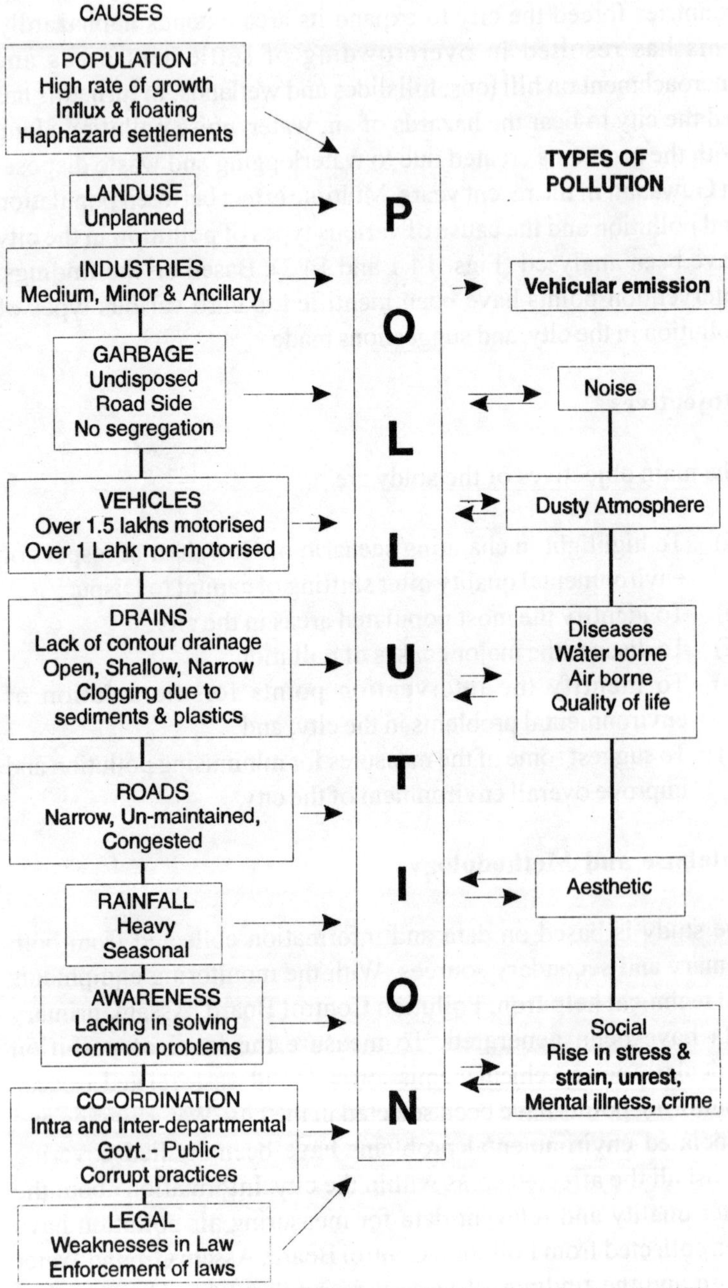

Fig. 14.1 : Pollution Related Problem in Guwahati City

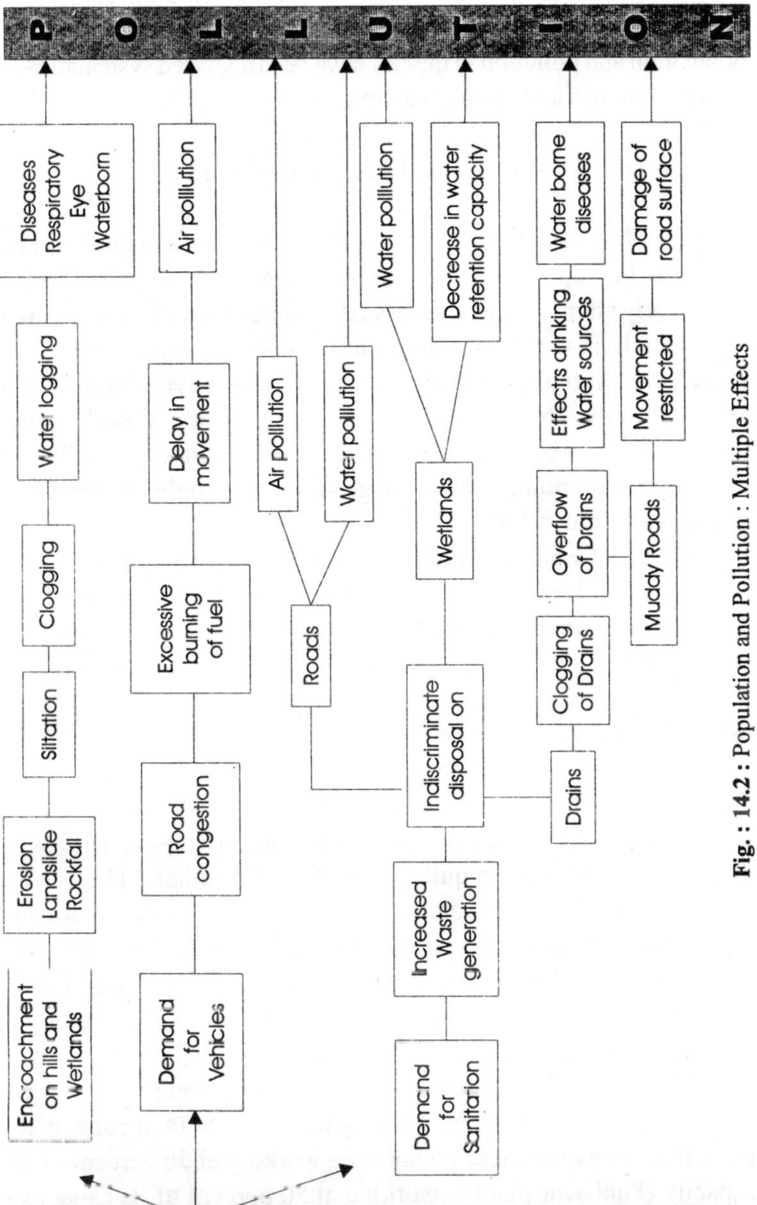

Fig. : 14.2 : Population and Pollution : Multiple Effects

obtained are presented in tables and diagrams and interpreted on the basis of standard norms. Moreover, multiple effect between population and pollution in the city have been analysed systematically using a few models and flowcharts.

Environmental Status and Level of Pollution

Guwahati has developed both in terms of quantity and quality. The increase in population has changed the natural environment particularly after 1972, as it necessitated a large number of residential units which in turn has required large built-up land at the cost of forest lands, agricultural land, hill slopes and low-lying lands in and around the city. The negative effects are soil erosion, waterlogging, landslides etc. which have ushered in new problems of pollution like garbage dumping, traffic congestion – as people, automobiles and services grow day by day.

Levels of water, air and noise pollution have been boosted up further by regular flow of people to the city in search of livelihood, which has contributed to the growth of slums and insanitary conditions.

Water Pollution

Polluted water at source is responsible for the outbreak of waterborne diseases such as typhoid, hepatitis, gestro-enteritis, skin diseases etc. Which are quite common in Guwahati. The city is facing serious drinking water problem. There are water treatment plants located at Panbazar, Satpukhuri, Gauhati University, Kamakhya Hills, Pandu, Guwahati Refinery and Hengrabari with a total capacity of 114,862 mld (million litres per day). Except for the treatment plant at Hengrabari which was installed by the Assam Urban Water Supply and Sewerage Board with financial assistance from HUDCO, all plants are working much below their capacities. Even if we consider these plants to be working at 50 percent of its capacity (Panbazar plant is working at 50 percent of its capacity) and the 25 percent as losses of distribution, only 68916 mld reaches the city population. Considering the standard supply norm for each person this quantity can satisfy the need of only 5.1 lakh people. As the city has 12 lakh (including 2 lakh floating) population around seven lakh people are deprived of getting treated water. As a result more than fifty percent of the population depend either on ground water or surface water sources. From the result of water quality analysis the surface water particularly the shallow tube well and well waters are not safe. The waste water from households, commercial and business establishments, small and medium industries within the city flow into the rivers like Bharalu, Brahmaputra, wetlands and low-lying areas (Lal & Bhattacharyya). As a result surface and well water in many parts of the city become unsafe for drinking, bathing and even washing purposes.

Air Pollution

Air Pollution in Guwahati has increased in recent years mainly due to overcrowding, indiscriminate hills cutting, waterlogging and unplanned growth of residential, commercial and industrial activities. Moreover, due to uneven topography, the geographical conditions and the climatic factors and elements like circulation of air, temperature, radiation level and alternate change of local low and high pressure gradient etc., all have a role in the growing concentration and unequal dispersion of the air pollutants within the city. Moreover, owing to the violation of certain rules related to localisation of industries, construction of houses, hill cutting etc. and negligence towards implementation of the "Master plan of the city" have severe impact on the dispersion of the air pollutants. The concentration of air pollution are also affected by the micro-level change in the atmosphere.

The pollutants which finds their way into the lower layers of atmosphere in the city are fine clay particles, dry organic matters of municipal waste, sulphur dioxide, carbon monoxide, unburnt hydrocarbon mixed with water vapour, a noxious mixture of fog and smoke and also miscellaneous pollutants. As the city is almost blocked on three sides by hills and hillocks, free movements of air is hampered, for which pollution level is comparatively higher in a few pockets.

The result of ambient air quality analysis of certain selected stations of greater Guwahati have been given in Table 14.1. It has been observed that in most cases SO_2 and NO_2 have been found below the prescribed limit, if the standard for area, under category A is considered. However, these two pollutants have been found more in all the points during the pre-monsoon season. This indicates that during the pre-monsoon season on account of the lack of rainfall or the limited quantity of rainfall the quantity of suspended particles is high. But in case of Adabari due to high traffic all the time the level of suspended particles is high not only in pre-monsoon season but throughout the year.

Table 14.1 : Result of Ambient Air Quality analysis of certain selected stations of greater Guwahati

(in micro gm/m³)

Area station	SO_2		NO_2		SPM	
	Pre-Monsoon	Monsoon	Pre-Monsoon	Monsoon	Pre-Monsoon	Monsoon
1	2	3	4	5	6	7
Dispur	34	12	57	19	317	154
Khanapara	31	6	56	15	167	54
Noonmati	6	22	32	18	259	59
Adabari	13	9	20	16	441	223
Dharapur	30	26	13	65	552	120
Airport	10	12	19	28	914	81
Amingaon	5	6	18	15	113	58
Beltola	6	21	16	22	238	151
Ulubari	8	9	17	23	290	82
Fatasil Ambari	36	32	29	44	232	60
Digheswari Temple	BDL	BDL	10	12	47	42

BDL : Below Detectable Limit.

Vehicular Emission

Vehicular emission is becoming a problem in the city. The number of motorised vehicles in Guwahati upto 1987 was around 80,000 which has now increased to almost double of this number. The registration record shows a very high rate of growth in all categories of motorised vehicles. The number of such vehicle in Guwahati have doubled in the last five years. Obviously, this rate of increase has caused more fuel consumption and consequently more emission in the atmosphere. Level being more with larger number of old and ill-maintained vehicles and use of inferior quality petrol.

Moreover, non-motorised vehicles are also increasing at an alarming rate. These slow moving vehicles on road and their parking at roadside cause resistance to the free movement of motorised vehicles and consequently cause more vehicular emission in the city. The vehicular emission survey (Tables 14.2 and 14.3) shows more than 80 percent of diesel vehicles and 53 percent of petrol vehicles in the city violate the standard emission limit. Narrow and unmaintained roads, frequent city buses plying on road and limitless haltage at some vital points create frequent traffic congestion. As a result the vehicles at frequent congestion points such as Ganeshguri, Ulubari, Paltanbazar, Chandmari, Silpukhuri, Guwahati Club, Ambari, Fancybazar, Tokobari areas the vehicles throw a high collective dose of air polluants into the environment.

Table 14.2 : Result of Vehicular Emission Survey at Guwahati Petrol Vehicles

Date	Station	No. of Vehicle Tested	No. of Vehicle exceeding Limit	P.C. of Violation
24-06-99	Maligaon	159	33	20.75
25-06-99	Ulubari	167	72	40.1
28-06-99	Near Meghdoot Cinema	147	72	48.9
29-06-99	Guwahati Club	230	163	70.8
02-07-99	Zoo Narengi Road	152	108	71.0
03-07-99	Ganeshguri	142	70	49.2
21-07-99	Kachari	112	70	52.5
	Total Average	1109	588	53

Source : PCBA.

Table 14.3 : Result of Vehicular Emission Survey at Guwahati Diesel Vehicles

Date	Station	No. of Vehicle Tested	No. of Vehicle exceeding Limit	P.C. of Violation
22-06-99	Amingaon	28	20	71.4
23-06-99	Adabari	69	62	89.8
02-07-99	Zoo Narengi Road	36	27	75.0
14-07-99	Khanapara	42	29	69.0
15-07-99	H.H. bypass (Beltola)	46	41	89.0
	Total Average	221	179	81.0

Source : PCBA.

Noise Pollution

The main source of noise in Guwahati, as in other cities of the world are automobiles, construction equipments, loud-speakers, bursting crackers etc. According to the Institute of Road Traffic Education (IRTE), Delhi is the noisiest city in India with 83 decibels (dB) against the accepted level of 77 dB at the maximum during the day time and 50 dB at night. Corresponding figures for Calcutta are 82 and 75, Mumbai 80 and 74 and Chennai 77 and 73. Guwahati too is not lagging behind. Guwahati being the gateway to north-east, people started experiencing high noise levels in the recent years mainly due to increase of automobiles. Rapid increase of population, vehicular traffic, mushroom growth of small industrial units and workshops and depletion of green cover are cumulatively causing noise population in the city. An intensive monitoring on noise level was done in collaboration with Pollution Control Board, Assam at various points and different environment results of which have been presented in Tables 14.4, 14.5 and 14.6.

Table 14.4 : Ambient noise level at different localities in Guwahati

Area	Location	dB recorded	Ambient noise standard limit in dB (A) Log
Commercial	1. Panbazar traffic point	75	65 at day time
	2. Fancybazar	65	
	3. Ganeshguri	78	
Residential & Commercial	4. Chandmari	80	55 at day time
	5. Silpukhuri	90	
	6. Guwahati Club	85	
Sensitive	7. High Court	78	50 at day time
	8. Cotton College	65	
	9. MMC Hospital	65	

Source : PCBA.

Table 14.5 : Average day time Noise Level in Educational Institute

Name of Institute	Noise Level (in dB)
Maligaon Railway Gate School	53 – 69
Ulubari Primary School	63 – 71
B. Barooah College	65 – 77
T.C. Girls School	56 – 66
St. Mary's School	61 – 85
Maharishi Vidya Mandir	58 – 67
J. B. Law College	66 – 72
Assam Engineering Institute	56 – 63
Gopal Boro H.S. School	59 – 65
Dispur College	60 – 70
Assam Textile Institute	56 – 69

Table 14.6 : Average day time Noise Level in Hospitals

Name of Hospital	Range of noise level	
	in campus (in dB)	in wards/Doctor's room (in dB)
Good Friend Hospital	75 – 77	68 – 70
Wintrobe Hospital	64 – 86	55 – 65
MMC Hospital	59 – 66	58 – 63
Polyclinic Hospital	61 – 64	58 – 63
Midland Clinic	74 – 86	69 – 80

Solid Waste and Waterlogging

Apart from the above two pollutants, solid waste and waterlogging are responsible for the increase of pollution in the city. From a study on Municipal Solid Waste (M. Rahman, 1995 an ASTE Council sponsored project) it has been found that Guwahati city generated 184 metric tones of solid waste everyday. Based on 1991 census, the garbage generation per head works out to be 0.3 kg per day and per household is 1461 kg. But with the increase in population the waste generation will also increase. By the end of the century, the waste generation will easily stand between 300 to 400 metric tonnes. So far most of the solid wastes generated in the city are organic in nature (78%). Non-degradable waste such as plastic and glass accounts only 8% of the total waste generated. But with changing life style of the people, it is posing a threat to the city with plastic materials thrown away by the citizen, clogging drains and increasing breeding ground for deadly germs. Run-off water from garbage with toxic substances infiltrate deep in the soil and pollutes the ground water too. Secondly, water logging is another tedious experience for the Guwahatians which is common in Chandmari, Bamunimaidan, Silpukhuri, Ambari, Guwahati Club, Lakhtokiya, Ganeshguri, Maligaon, Geetanagar, Gandhibasti, Nabin Nagar, Christian Basti areas. Heavy seasonal rainfall, exposed hill slopes, defective drainage network, hill cutting for construction purposes, encroachment in low-lying areas and wetlands are the major causes of waterlogging and siltation in the above mentioned areas (P. Sharma 1998, AS TE Council sponsored project). The problem is becoming serious day by day. The waterlogging and siltation leads to dusty atmosphere and cause acute air pollution particularly after each heavy shower followed by sunshine.

Intervention Points

The pollution related issue have often been discussed in many forums. But in all the attempts a peacemeal approach has been taken for which many of the recommendations still remained to be implemented. In this study, a holistic approach has been taken and some of the intervention points are identified and a few suggestive measures have been put forth under the following heads.

Solid Waste Management

- Segregation of solid waste at source is required to facilitate recycling and materialise linkage between formal and informal sectors.
- Collection of solid waste at fixed times from households must be done for systematic disposal. Non-motorised vehicles could be used in the bylanes.
- Disposing or throwing of garbage in places other than the provisions of the laws should be punishable with fine.
- In similar lines with Delhi or Mumbai, impetus has to be given to the private sector for participating the biological processing of Municipal domestic wastes.
- Use of polythene bags must be stopped and bigger sturdy bags manufactured for reuse.
- Since organic waste is more than 50%, dumping ground itself should have a vermicompost site, and the compost would be used as manure.

Traffic Management

- Private buses and cars should not be allowed to use the main road for parking and washing. One can use the Police Act, 1934.
- Multistoried parking space needs to be given top priority. These will not only eliminate road blocks due to parking but will also generate revenue for the Municipal Corporation.
- Proper parking space needs to be there, when one buys a truck or bus. A permit should be given provided the owner has his/her own parking space. This should be mandatory, violation of this will result in cancellation of road permit.

Housing, Landuse and Drainage

- Government should build housing colony for the slum and squatter dwellers to eradicate slums.
- Hill cutting should be stopped immediately. Truck found to carry red soil should be stopped and be punished.
- Encroachment in low-lying areas, roadsides and hilltops needs to be stopped immediately. Pavements must be cleared for pedestrians especially in Fancy Bazar, Paltan Bazar, Ganeshguri etc. There should be provision for separate lanes for bicycles and rickshaws.

Awareness and Social Responsibility

- Citizens, groups and local resident need to be channellised into civic projects for abatement of pollution. It should not be done in a mechanical way. Ownership of project must be there.
- The private sector needs to be roped into the beautification of the city.
- Schools and Colleges must be given impetus for activities involving environmental projects.
- It should be made mandatory for every shop to have its own bins.
- Pay and use facilities like toilets must be introduced and open air defecation should be prevented, if required heavy penalty levied for doing so.
- Black topping of roads till the edge is required for optimum use.

References

Bora, C.C. 1995, Noise Pollution; A general Overview, *News Letter*, Assam Pollution Control Board, pp. 12-13.

Bhattacharyya, B.K. (Ed) 1988, *Problems of Urban Development in Guwahati*, Omsons Pub., New Delhi, pp. 13-29.

Goswami, D.C. 1993, *Assam's Land Resources – A Satellite*

Based ARSAC Survey, Assam Sc. Soc. Guwahati p. 23.

Lal, P.C. and Bhattacharyya, K.G., 1989, A Short Term Study on the pollutional status of the Bharalu River, *J. Assam Sc. Soc.* 31 (2) pp. 1 – 9.

Pollution Control Board, Assam & Society for Research Development and Communication 1999, A Report Prepared for Ministry of Environment and Forests, Govt. of India, New Delhi.

15

GUWAHATI
A Hub of Industrial and Commercial Buoyancy of the North-East India

Monalisa Choudhury & Nayan Barua

Pragjyotishpura, the capital of ancient Kamrupa, which is today designated as Guwahati has witnessed tremendous changes both in its geographical boundary and in its socio-economic upheaval. Till today, three successive events, namely the establishment of Gauhati Refinery in 1962, the construction of a bridge over the river Brahmaputra at Saraighat in 1964 and the shifting of the capital of Assam from Shillong to Guwahati in 1973 had brought about far reaching impact upon social, economic and political life of Gauhatians. The city has become the hub of industrial and commercial activities not only for Assam but also for the entire North Eastern part of India. It is also being contemplated to be the future gateway of India's trade linkage with the South East Asia. The city with its population of nearly two million offers tremendous potentialities for growth of trade and commerce. This is being manifestated in the spurt of its commercial and industrial activities in the last three decades.

Transport Related Development

The speedy growth of population together with trade and industry has cast a boom over the development of transport business in the city. The road transport services to and from the city have made it the central point of business for the north-eastern region. The construction of broad gauge railway lines and the decision to accord international status to the Borjhar Airport have tremendous impact over the development of the city. Moreover, the intracity transport services have telling effect upon development of transport business in the city. Nearly 400 ordinary city buses and 80 deluxe super buses ceaselessly provide services to the commuters everyday. Besides the buses, the private taxies the autorickshaws and rickshaws have been plying everyday from one corner of the city to the other. The city bus business is organised by a couple of transport organisations, *viz.* the Greater Guwahati Motor Transport Association, Guwahati Deluxe Bus Owners' Association and the Greater Guwahati Motor Bus Owners' Association. Moreover, inter-district day and night bus services are also available from the Paltanbazar and Adabari area of the city. Nearly ten to twenty thousand commuters travel daily in these buses. The parallel broadgauge line which has been recently completed in the South Bank of the river Brahmaputra is likely to boost up trade connection with the rest of India. The buoyancy in the transport business has led to the growth of many subsidiary business like Motor Vehicles body building industry, weigh bridge, fuel depot repairing and refuelling centres etc.

Industrial Growth

The establishment of the Gauhati Refinery in 1962 may be considered as the first major debut of the city in the field of industrialisation. It occupies approximately an area of 14.7 acres with its three process units, a captive power point, crude and product storage, product blending and the other offside facilities.

The Gauhati Refinery produces Reformer Naphtha (RN),

Motor Spirit (MS), Aviation Tri Fuel (ATF), Superior Kerosene Oil (SKO), High Speed Diesel (HSD), Light Diesel Oil (LDO), Funance Oil (FO), Low Sulpher Heavy Stock (LSHS), Liquefied Petroleum Gas (LPG), Raw Petroleum Coke (LPC). The finish products are despatched from the refinery locally by the train wagons and tank lorries to meet the requirement of North-East.

Another oldest industrial unit located in the heart of the city is the Assam Carbon Products Limited. It produces Carbon block from the raw petroleum coke of Gauhati Refinery. The India Carbon Products Limited is located at the eastern end of the city. There is a Liquefied Petroleum Gas (LPG) bottling plant at North Guwahati. The Industrial township of the city has also grown-up in the southern part along the National Highway. There are innumerable chemical based, iron based, cement based and agro-based units engaged in the production of various consumer and plant needed goods. Besides these, there are innumerable factories of small size, operating within the city. It is worth mentioning that 70 percent of the total registered factories of the district (i.e. 485) are alone situated within the city. Besides a substantial number of small scale registered units of Kamrup district (7846) are also located within the municipal area of the city.

The Gauhati Stock Exchange Limited

Another very significant step in the development of trade and industry of the North-East is the establishment of Gauhati Stock Exchange in the year 1983. The stock exchange is located in the heart of the Guwahati city at the Saraf Building, A.T. Road. It was recognised by the Ministry of Finance, Government of India in 1984.

Though at present 288 companies with paid up capital of Rs. 4254 crores have been listed in the exchange, yet the activities of the Gauhati Stock Exchange is totally stopped from June,1999 due to devastating fire which occurred in the same year destroying the whole of the computer section of the exchange. Although restoration work is going on at present but the same is likely to take longer time owing to the fact that the activities of the exchange have not been smooth ever since the great securities scam in the year 1990. In the near future, the Gauhati Stock Exchange Limited is likely to stop operating as a recongnised Stock Exchange and may merge with the National Stock Exchange, Bombay for which discussion are going on among the authorities.

The Guwahati Tea Auction Centre

The establishment of the Guwahati Tea Auction Centre (GTAC) also has a great impact on the business scenario of the Guwahati City. The centre was established on September 25, 1970. It is located on the G.S. Road, Dispur Guwahati.

The membership of GTAC presently stands at 921 which include 586 tea estates, 292 buyers, 9 brokers and 34 warehouses. The procedure of auction is conducted as per Guwahati Tea Auction Centre Rules and the directives from the tea board.

Assam is the largest tea producing state in India producing nearly fifty percent of the tea produced in the country. The Guwahati Tea Auction Centre has not only extended help to the tea producers of Assam but also provided scope of employment and has been a major source of income to the State Government. With the establishment of the auction centre at Guwahati and several other anciliary organisations like tea broking firms, tea warehouses, transport agencies, the Inland Container Depot the unemployment problem of Assam particularly of Guwahati has been solved to a large extent.

Moreover, the establishment of North-East Frontier Railway's Inland Container Depot (ICD) at Amingaon in 1986 opened a new era in the marketing of tea and also other agricultural commodities in the North-Eastern Region. The establishment of ICD placed due importance to the Guwahati Tea Auction Centre because all the facilities needed for export were available. The dry port facility for shipment of export cargo would prove to be economical to the users as compared to conventional means of overseas destinations. The significant benefits were by way of prevention of loss and damage in handling and transit speedier movement and quicker completion of customers and other facilities. Tea containers sent by train from the ICD were directly put on the mother vessel at Haldia Airport.

Animal Food Product in Guwahati

Guwahati city also has a very big wholesale fish market in the name of Paltanbazar Wholesale Fish Market Association. Established in the year 1997-98, it is one of the biggest wholesale fish market of the North-Eastern Region. At present there are 65 members of the association with nearly 1000 employees. Though the market mainly gives supply to the Greater Guwahati area yet a part of it is send to Latumbai and Tura in the State of Meghalaya. The average daily supply of fish to the market is 2 trucks, each containing 140 trays of 35 kg. each. The price of the fish depends upon the demand of the item. The peak season for sale is from the month of January to the month of June. The main places from where the supply come from are Lucknow, Howrah, Andhra Pradesh, Kanpur, Gandhinagar, Delhi, Bihar and also from Bangladesh (Elish).

Besides this, there is also a wholesale fish market of local fish of river Brahmaputra at the Uzanbazar area of the city. It is one of the oldest wholesale fish market of the city.

Moreover, the Guwahati City also has a wholesale Goat market in the Machkhowa area of the city but the market is not an organised one. Furthermore, dairy and poultry trade are also concentrated mostly on the outskirts of the city but in an unorganised manner. However, the West Guwahati Co-operative Milk Society situated at the Panjabari area of the city is an organised unit producing dairy products under the brand name '*Purabi*'.

Growth of Other Business

The building business in Guwahati City is also in its developing stage. Today in almost every locality there lies a sky touching apartment complex in Guwahati. The construction of apartment business started in Guwahati in the year 1986 when the first building organisation under the name of "Arunodoi" was formed. This organisation constructed its first apartment complex named "Arunodoi" at the Sarumotoria area of the city. Ever since then, many building organisations were formed. At present the number of such builders in the city is nearly about 100.

Besides this, the hotel industry is growing at a very high rate in the city. At present there are many two to three star hotels in Guwahati. Among them the hotel Brahmaputra Ashok, Hotel Belleview, Hotel Dynasty, Hotel Rajmahal, Hotel Rituraj are worth mentioning. The number of three star hotels in the city stands nearly 8. Moreover, there are many hotels meant for the middle and lower class people. There are also many restaurants in the city, the condition of some of which are very unhygenic.

Furthermore, there is also a mushroom growth of nursing homes in Guwahati City. These nursing homes can be categorically divided for high, middle and lower class people in respect of expenses. Besides, a few such nursing homes the others are meant for middle and lower class people. Among the most outstanding ones are the Guwahati Neurological Research Institute, Down Town Hospital, etc.

The Guwahati City also witnesses thousands of street vendors, hawkers, petty traders throughout the city. These businessmen are mostly found in the stuffy Paltanbazar, Fancy Bazar, Ulubari, Ganeshguri area of the city. The city also witnesses many wine shops the numbers of which at present extends to 250. Moreover, the city also witnesses a very big weekly market at the Beltola area of the city. This market is held twice a week on Sunday and Thursday. All types of commodities from vegetables, fish, meat, stationary items and readymade garments are sold in this market.

Furthermore, there is also a wholesale vegetable market at the Machkhowa area of the city.

Another flourishing business in Guwahati City is the running of Public Call Offices (PCO). Today, the Public Call Offices are found in almost every locality of the city. At present there are 2162 numbers of PCO operating in the city.

Besides this, today the beauty parlours are also doing very

good business in Guwahati. The first beauty parlour of the city was started in the Dighalipukhuri area of the city in the year 1979 under the name of Ritus Beauty Parlour. Consequently, many beauty parlours were opened in different parts of the city the number of which at present raises from four to five hundred.

Moreover, the private educational institutions are also growing up at an alarming rate in Guwahati. Besides the missionaries, the local people have also started many schools and Junior colleges in the city. There are also many vocational institutions in the city which imparts various types of courses.

Furthermore there are a number of institutions imparting computer coaching in the city which is a good source of income for many Guwahatians running such institutions. At present, there are about two hundred such institutes operating in the city.

There are also many industrial units in and around Guwahati mostly in the Bamunimaidan industrial area, Bonda Industrial area and in Amingaon. Further, there are many quarries and marble industries in and around the city.

Therefore, Guwahati in recent times have become a very important trade centre not only for the north-eastern region but also for the entire country. Although trade and commerce conferred a respectable status to Guwahati among the commercial capitals of the country, yet the unplanned and haphazard growth of many industries have contributed to its pollution also. There is no regular collection of industrial and commercial wastes by the civic authorities which has made the city's look ghastly and unhealthy. The pollution level have greatly affected the health of the people owing to excessive noise, smoke, and undisposed industrial effluents.

Therefore, it is high time that a full-fledged plan of action should be evolved to provide necessary infrastructure commensurate to the population and trade expansion of the city.

16

THE PRESENT CAPITAL PROJECT OF ASSAM

B. Datta Ray

Guwahati prior to 1972 had never been the political Head Quarters neither of the Ahoms nor of the British. The capital of Assan during Ahom period was Sivsagar. Guwahati was merely a mufassil station and had no claim over other places in the state by population or trade. David Scott had his heart fixed at Nonglow in the Khasi Hills for strategic reason which became his first Head Quarters at the conclusion of Khasi Wars. When Major White visited Nonglow in the middle of 1828, he found European fruit trees and bungalows constructed there. Everything promised a permanent stay there. The early death of Scott at Cherrapunjee on August 20, 1831 frustrated his dream. His successors were W. Cracraft, T.C. Robertson and Col. F. Jenkins. Jenkins held the longest term of office of Commissioner and Agent to the Governor General on the North-East India from February 1834 to February 1861. He was not interested for fixing his Head Quarters of Assam in any plains station. Jenkins had his Head Quarters in a boat, having always moved about and spent most of his time on the river Brahmaputra. It is certain that the first three Commissioners of Assam never thought of making Guwahati their Head Quarters. Robertson was even more careful in avoiding Guwahati.

Col. Henry Hopkinson who succeeded Jenkins in March 1861, held his office as Commissioner of Assam till the creation of new Chief Commssionership in 1874. Guwahati was considered to be insanitory to be the political Head Quarters of the province of Assam. Col. Hopkinson in his report in 1866 wrote on the unsuitability of Guwahati. He wrote though it had little to recommend beyond its geographical position, its extreme insalubrity must baffle any attempt to make it the efficient Head Quarters of Assam division. Guwahati is bounded on one side by the river Brahmaputra, on another side by a malarious marsh and on other sides by the hills. The Chief Engineer reported that the only sites available for building new houses were a few open spaces left in the town, which it would be pity to occupy. Climate was sufficient to recommend Shillong in preference to Guwahati to become the political Head Quarters of the province of Assam in 1874. No paper could as yet been traced fixing Guwahati as the Head Quarters during the British period. No Commissioner had any authority for fixing his Head Quarters at Guwahati. The Governor General on 29th May, 1874 approved of the selection of Shillong by Col. R. H. Keatinge to be the Head Quarters of the Chief Commisisionership of Assam who after staying barely forty days shifted his Head Quarters to Shillong, the dream child of Col. Hopkinson.

A new situation arose in 1972 with the emergence of Meghalaya as a full state. It needed a political decision for shifting the Head Quarters from Shillong to Guwahati. The nearest station to Shillong was Guwahati, and rows of very temporary structures were erected on a war footing by the Sarat Chandra Sinha Government and by 1974-75 offices started moving to a sleepy village site amidst paddy fields to be the political Head Quarters of Assam, however, temporarily it might have been. Dharmananda Das, the then Chief Secretary to the Assam Government was in charge of the project to built overnight the township of Dispur. But no ecological studies were made for such an hasty decision which had now affected the life and living of the people of Greater Guwahati. In 1983-85 during the first Chief Ministership of Hiteswar Saikia a decision was taken to build the permanent capital of Assam at Chandrapur about 25 km east of Guwahati in a low hilly healthy terrain with a sound possibilities of building a modern capital city like Chandigarh. But it appears now that vested interest had now almost scuttled the Chandrapur capital project. This is a pity. At Dispur, air pollution because of suspended particles in the air, is heavy in the pre-monsoon days, so also at the nearby Beltola and Khanapara region.

Guwahati is facing an escalating trend of air pollution. According to Assam Pollution Controal Board report during pre-monsoon 1994, in 11 selected stations including Dispur, Khanapara, Noonmati, Adabari, Dharapur, Airport, Amingaon, Beltola, Ulubari, Fatasil, Ambari and Digheswari temple, revealed that the dispersion of the pollutants, SO_2, NO_2 and SPM in the city was not uniform and it varied from season to season and from area to area.

Though the pollutants of SO_2 and NO_2 have not exceeded the prescribed limits in the residential and rural areas of the city, in several cases SPM crossed the prescribed limits during the pre-monsoon season, at Adabari, Dharapur, Dispur and Beltola. This indicated that during the pre-monsoon season, on account of the lack of rainfall or for the limited quantity of rainfall, the atmosphere contains sufficient quantity of suspended particles. Adabari receives a higher amount of suspended particles because of the buses at the bus terminal emitting significant amount of suspended articles. SPM exceed the prescribed limit at Dispur, Dharapur and Beltola during the monsoon as well.

The sensitive areas of the city like Dispur, Khanapara, Dharapur and Fatasil, Ambari area are facing air pollution over the prescribed limits of SO_2 during both the pre-monsoon and monsoon period. Moreover, the contents of Oxides of Nitrogen have also crossed the limits at Dispur, Khanapara and Noonmati during the pre-monsoon and at Dharapur and Fatasil, Ambari areas during monsoon time.

The population of Guwahati has increased from about 50,000 in the fifties to about 1.5 million at present. A small sleepy mufassil town in the fifties with innumerable ponds, water bodies in it, has grown into a major urban population concentration in north-east India in less than half of a century and would mark at least 2 million figure in two decades time. This unplanned growth of Guwahati has created serious ecological imbalance such as water logging as indicative. There is neither an underground swerage line nor an overground drainage facility leading to serious health hazards and mosquito menace. It has encroached upon open spaces, green grasslands, paddy fields and water bodies upsetting urban ecological balance. We do not know much of urban ecology. Ecology deals with varied inter-relationship that exist between different inter-dependent components of environment. Such components are plants, forests, micro-organism, air, water bodies climate and' physical structures of the habitat each of the components influencing the nature of the properties and functioning of the other for the maintenance and furtherance of life. The growth of the urban centre like that of Guwahati should be in harmony with the ecological balance. Eco-development should be the approach to all urban development.

The unplanned human settlements in and around Guwahati have led to flash floods, landslides and waterlogging everywhere in around Guwahati. Every piece of habitable land including low hills around the city bears the testimony of such disastrous growth. Forest development in and around the city is required as the forest cover is the source of oxygen, water and soil protection and regeneration. Urban development should take into consideration the environment issues fully participated by the people of the human settlement to make the urban areas safe for living. The choice of Guwahati as the political and administrative Head Quarter is, as it stands today, is an ecological disaster.

17

EDUCATION OF STREET CHILDREN IN GREATER GUWAHATI
Problems and Prospects

Gayatree Goswamee

Every child has the right to free primary education says Article 28 of the UN convention on the Rights of the child. In 1986, the National Policy on Education had vowed to provide free and compulsory education to all children upto the age of 14 before the 21st century. In reality, the picture is that India has entered the new millennium with the largest number of illiterates in the world. For millions of children who do not know where there next meal will come from, education is perhaps a luxury they can afford.

It is not something rare to see a poverty stricken child in any city or urban area loitering, working or living on the streets, market places, railway station or any other public place, but what really struck me was the attitude towards life of such a street child. "I had to resort to ragpicking to help my family after my father died", confessed 11year old Salima wearing a torn frock with unruly hair. I asked her why she did not go to school. To this, she answered

"Will books give me my daily bread? Moreover, where is the time?" After helping her mother in her household chores she has to go with her friends for rag picking during the day time. Accordingly to Salima going to school is a sheer waste of time.

The problem of street children is assuming serious proportion in the urban centers throughout the world. Given as they are to a wandering life style, no survey can provide an accurate estimate of its numbers. Alienated and insulated by society, such children suffer from low self-esteem. The UNICEF by dividing the street children into two co-existing categories as those "On the street" (who keeps some link with their families) and those "of the street" (who are totally on their own) finds the presence of over thirty million street children in the world of whom 30% might be on their own, the rest being with their families.

The Need of an Exploratory Study in Greater Guwahati

Guwahati is the nerve centre of the North East and it has became the hub of business, industrial and commercial activities. With the rapid pace of urbanisation there is also, like the urban centres elsewhere a rapid increase in the number of street children in the city. Boys and girls clad in torn and dirty shreds with huge gunny bags on their back, undernourished, scouring the Guwahati Municipal Corporation dustbins and the garbage heaps is a common sight in the city of Guwahati. One finds them ererywhere–In Fancybazar, Panbazar, Silpukhuri, Chandmari, Chenikuthi, Ganeshguri, Beltola – everywhere. They are least bothered about who is around them or watching them. Their only concern is to get "Maal" a term used for the materials these children collect. The materials they collect are pieces of paper, plastic bits, metal pieces, bottles etc. They earn Rs. 10 to Rs. 100 per day selling these materials. These children are also engaged in diverse occupations like working in workshops, tea-stalls, roadside eating places, garages, begging, stealing, pick-pocketing etc. at this tender age. Consequently, they are robbed of their childhood, are exploited and much of their potentials remain untapped and unexplored. Therefore, there is an urgent need to identify and channelise their immense energy and talents by providing right direction through right education.

Street Children Population in Guwahati

Till date no extensive study has been conducted to assess the total number of street children population in Greater Guwahati. (They lead a wandering life style and comprise a transit population moving from place to place looking for a secure place because they often face the wrath of Railway Authorities and other Government Agencies). The only survey available was done by the Indian Council of Child Welfare, Ambari, Guwahati during the year 1994.

Educational Facilities Available to the Street Children in Greater Guwahati

It is observed that quite a number of social welfare organisation, associations, clubs, missionaries etc. are devoting their efforts for the upliftment of the street children.

Mention may be made of two prominent organisations in Guwahati, namely, the Indian Council for Child Welfare and the World Vision of India. The ICCW has been running six centres for the street children under the Street Children Project or the Suraj Mukhi Sishu Kalyan Kendras (Since December 1994). These centres are namely:

(1) Kalibari (Near Railway Station).
(2) Arya Nagar (Near Arya Vidyapith College).
(3) Birubari (Ram Krishna Mission Road).
(4) Mothgoria (Noonmati).
(5) Bhetapara (Hatigaon).
(6) Sivanagar (Hengrabari).

Children are identified from vulnerable places after a survey. The children are selected from the age-group 6 to 16 years. There are 50 children in each centre. (This is the target population as laid down by the Ministry of Welfare, Government of India.)

The other project has been undertaken by the World Vision Organisation whose project is titled 'Gauhati Street Children Project'. It was started in May 1996 and a centre for the education of the street children in the Silpukhuri area of the city. This centre was started with the aim of making a difference in the lives of the children living in the railway track areas through health, education and awareness programmes. It gathers, educates and provides guidance and counselling to street children and their parents for better and healthy living.

Another centre has been recently started last year (1999) in the Bamunimaidan area of the city.

The organisations working for the upliftment of the street children face several difficulties. Some major problems are–

(a) Lack of funds.
(b) Lack of trained personnel with specialised skills to work for the street children.
(c) Non-availability of suitable accommodation and other infrastructural facilities to run the centre.
(d) Apathy of the Government and the public at large.
(e) Children refuse to come to school. They have to be collected from their houses and the neighbouring areas.

The organization working for the street children in Greater Guwahati are providing the following :–

(1) Special non-formal schooling facilities for children who have no opportunity to attend formal school because of poverty.
(2) Vocational training opportunities for such children. They are taught cutting, stitching, umbrella repairing, jute making, car repairing etc. Vocational trainers have been appointed in each centre and the vocational training starts from 1 p.m. to 3.30 p.m.
(3) Organises home visits regularly to motivate and encourage the parents to send their children to school to read and write instead of rag-picking.
(4) Provides health check-up for all children by an experienced physician.

(5) Provides special attention to the adolescent girls to protect them from exploitation, mainly sexual exploitation.

(6) Assisting children to get themselves enrolled in formal schools.

(7) Assisting children to find suitable employment after education and training.

(8) Provides recreational facilities such as songs, rhymes and dances. Different outdoor and indoor games are also played – the carrom board being very popular among the children. Sometimes the children are taken to the zoo or the park for educational and recreational activities.

(9) Community Awareness meetings are arranged periodically and vital issues regarding family planning, nutrition, cleanliness, diseases etc. are discussed with the parents.

Suggestions for improving the Educational Facilities of the Street Children

1. *Recruitment of Trained Personnel :* All street children educators should be properly trained. They should also be proficient in disciplines like child psychology and social work.
2. *Creation of Public Awareness :* Extensive use of mass media, the press, television and radio can create public awareness about the problem of street children and develop positive attitude towards them.
3. *Infrastructural Facilities :* The Government should come forward to set up separate institutions exclusively for the education of the street children. Some of the existing school buildings in the city can be used to conduct the activities for the welfare of the street children especially when the normal school hours are over.
4. *Recreational and Cultural Facilities :* Different types of recreational and cultural activities are essential for the development of a child's personality. Unfortunately, the street child is robbed of from these facilities. Under such circumstances, it is imperative that the curriculum should allot time for such activities.

5. *Evening Classes and Holiday Schools* : Many of the street children have to go out during the day time to earn and support their families. Therefore, in order to suit these children evening classes and holiday schools are needed to be established.
6. *Educational Tours and Camps* : Field trips and excursions will enable the street children to enhance their knowledge and outlook.
7. *Moral Education* : The unhealthy environment at home negatively affects the child. To develop a positive attitude in the child towards the family and the society at large, it is necessary that education on morals and values be imparted to the street child.
8. *Vocational Training* : Training in different vocations will develop their knowledge and skill in different vocational fields and this will in due course of time help the street children in getting employment. Training in various handicrafts, weaving, knitting, embroidery, cycle and motor vehicle repairing, printing, book binding, tailoring, etc. will contribute a lot in making them suitable for employment in different occupations.
9. *Cheanliness Drives* : The street children should be taught about the benefits of sound health and hygiene. Self-awareness can be created by conducting cleanliness drives in and around the centres and also in their localities. A number of street children have been found to indulge themselves in smoking, chewing tobacco, consumption of alcohol and drugs at a very tender age. In order to check this it is necessary that the street educators enlighten these children and their parents regarding the evil effects of drugs and alcohol.

Conclusion

Problems of street children are many. These can be minimized only through the concerted efforts of the public, the Government, the Non-governmental organisations, teachers and the community at large. With its growing magnitude, there is an urgent need to increase our sensitivity and commitment to meaningful action on the survival, protection and development of street children.

18

STREET FOOD VENDING IN GUWAHATI
Problems and Prospects

Mini Bhattacharyya Thakur

The selling of ready-to-eat food along the streets is an ubiquitous activity in many cities around the world. Street food vending implies the activities related to the making, selling and eating of food on the streets. Such food includes anything sold on the street that can be eaten without further processing (Tinker 1987). Street food encompasses all types of edible: relishes, snacks, sweet-meats, fruits, beverages and even meals. They are sold from temporary sheds and shops on the roadside, pushcarts or by moving from locality to locality. They are seen near market places, city bus stops, cinema halls and sometimes in street corners along busy thorough- fares in commercial, residential and office areas.

Street food vending is an important part of modern life which serves two vital functions. First, it serves food quickly and cheaply to a large section of urban dwellers and visitors. Secondly, it provides employment to a number of people who do not have educational qualification or skill for formal sector employment.

This study deals with the activity of street food vending in Guwahati city and its associated problems and relevant issues.

Street food vending is relativity a new phenomenon in Guwahati, prevalent only since the last three to four decades. Earlier, eating of cooked food (particularly among the Hindus) was largely confined to the domestic hearth an area of purity and sanctity. Home was usually the place for eating food. Partaking of cooked food outside home where the social background and the caste of the cook are unknown was restricted. However, progressive urbanisation and industrialisation since about the 1950s have led to the growth of a cosmopolitan culture through migration of diverse groups of people and the need to eat in an urban area cheaply, and quickly have led to the emergence of the street food (Bhattacharyya 1997).

As the largest urban and commercial centre in the north-east India, Guwahati attracts thousands of visitors, traders, businessmen and workers from both within and outside the state contributing to the tremendous increase in population from 2,52,305 in 1971 to 5,84,342 in 1991. Adding to the already existing population, there is a daily inflow of a large number of people from neighbouring villages, towns and districts to the city. It is this transient section of people along with the workers, travellers and men without families who create the demand for quick and cheap ready-to-eat street food.

The Food Vendors

The vendors are middle aged men and women (mediam age: 33.08 years) who are from diverse regional, linguistic, religious, caste and socio-cultural backgrounds. They do not belong to one homogeneous social group. They are primarily rural migrants hailing from the states of Bihar, West Bengal and Assam. The percentage of male vendors in Guwahati outnumber female sellers. In a sample of 360 vendors 14 (3.9%) are women. The majority of vendors are Hindus (96%) from different caste groups, the rest are Muslims.

The educational attainment of the vendors are low 34.4% are illiterate and 21.1% are barely literate who can sign their names. From the vendors who have got formal schooling, 28.9% have studied upto primary level, 9.7% reached middle level and 5.5% have studied upto high school including 5 persons who have completed high school. Out of 360 vendors, only one person (0.27%) has completed graduation and there are no vendor with technical or non-technical degree, diploma or certificates.

The street food vendors of Guwahati sell as many as 55 varieties of food and snacks in locations which are easily approachable and attract a large number of customers (see Fig.18.1). Bus stops, railway station, cinema halls, parks, market places, hospitals, courts and Government offices are prized locations. The sellers of street food are both stationary and mobile. The stationary vendors are those who sell them from a fixed location throughout the day. They sell from shops, stalls or cart (rendered stationary by removing the wheels). They usually sell tea, snacks (salted and sweets), *pulao*, chowmein, *roti-sabji* and meals (both vegetarian and non-vegetarian). These vendors prepare the food to be coocked in the site itself and many of these sellers have some kind of temporary sitting arrangement. But space is limited and the tendency of vendors to spill over and block roads or pavement is highly likely as in areas A, B & F cited in (Fig.18.1). In addition the narrow size of roads in the city (except for a few main roads), coupled with heavy traffic including the slow moving vehicles, commuters and absence of proper footpaths (often broken and clogged) adds to congestion.

In contrast, the mobile sellers sell by shuffling from one location to another during the day and in the evening, sell in a busy intersection of a market place. They sell different kinds of relishes like *chanachur*, *jhalmuri*, sweetmeats, fruits slices, etc. from boxes, trays, small ambulatory carts or carrying poles.

The Trade

Vending outlets are primarily one-man units (82%). However, home help from wife and children are utilised by 73.4 per- cent of vendors while 23 per cent hire workers on a regular or seasonal basis. Friends contribute 3.6 per cent of labour. Personal savings form the highest source of starting capital (55.83%) followed by family source (20.28%) and friends (15.56%). Loans from bank are not popular because of complicated paperwork and procedures.

Vendors largely depend upon daily credit to buy the raw materials. Many felt that their costs would be reduced if they could buy in bulk, but capital is a major problem for many vendors. Despite having an average income of Rs.50.00 per day (1991 estimate)

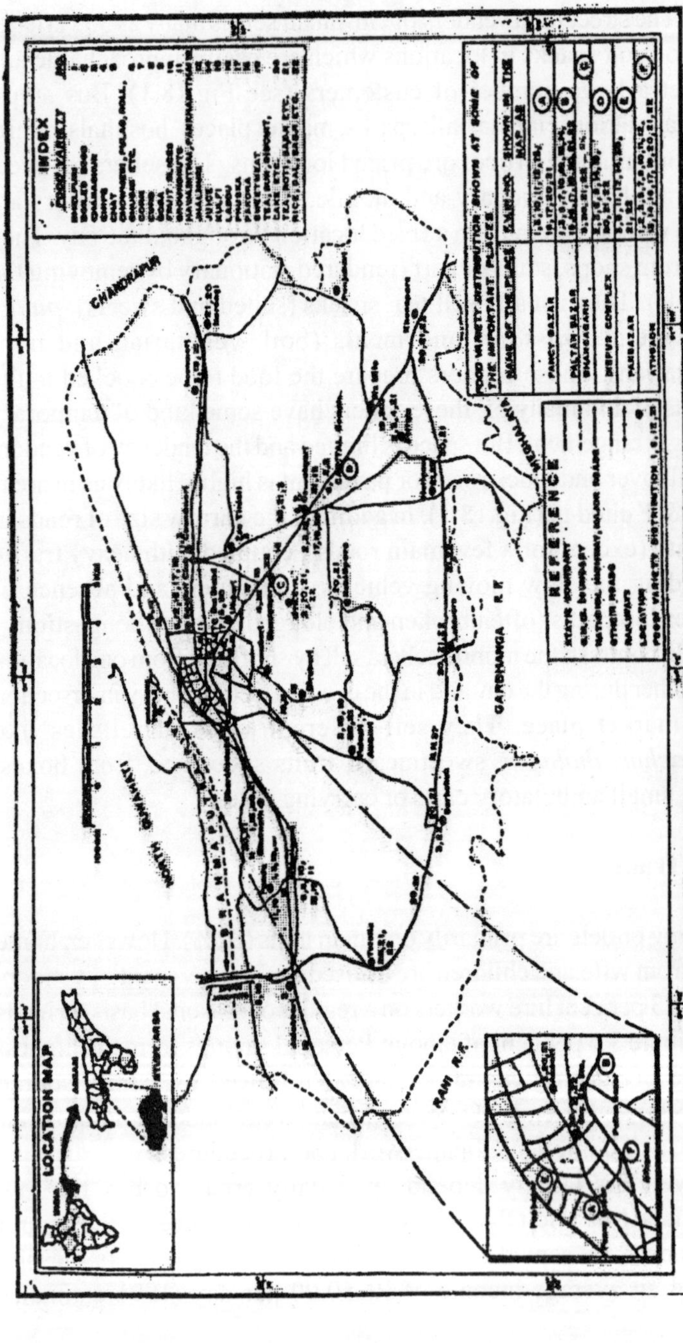

Fig. 18.1 : Map of Guwahati City, Assam, Showing Distribution of Sreet Food Variety, 1991

few vendors seem eager to expand in this trade. Instead they send home money to be utilised on education of their children and maintenance of family. One of the major factors which restricts expansion is the "risk" of operating without a valid trade licence. The Guwahati Municipal Corporation tries to control street food vending by making licences for trading mandatory. In Guwahati, a small section (10.5%) of sellers had licences at the time of study. These vendors include mobile sellers of *chanachur*, *phuska* (kind of relish), sugarcane juice pressers and a few stationary food sellers who own pushcarts. But the licences are for the pushcarts as slow moving vehicles and not for vending street food as such.

Street Food Vending and Municipal Control

Selling of food on the street is illegal in most countries and hawkers and venders employed in offering this essential service are objects of antipathy. Often, the presence of street food is seen as a sign of Third World backwardness to be removed. The visit of dignitaries to the city, decision to enforce law against illegal structures, road widening or the spread of epidemic disease bring stringent control upon all who sell ready-to-eat food. The Municipality thus concentrates on cleaning up the streets while ignoring the importance of street food as urban food. The argument that street food are sold under unsanitary conditions has long been used by the government as an excuse for eliminating them. Cooked food consumed soon after preparation is usually safe; contamination comes from dust and flies settling on uncovered food (Tinker 1997:89),Guwahati requires all food to be covered. However, a major health problem is access to clean water for cooking, washing and drinking. 82.9 per cent of food vendors in Guwahati have access to tap water but not available throughout the day or in all areas of the city. Water is required to be stored and often kept in dirty drums. Others use water from wells, tube-wells, pond and even rain water.

Control of street food and quality of food sold are often justified on grounds of health. But imposition of strict health codes often results in bribery rather than improved hygiene. Awareness of health hazard and improved hygienic standards in dealing with cooked food on the part of vendors will improve the safety of street food to a great extent. In addition, regular inspection by Municipal workers will elevate street food standard.

In Guwahati, harassment of food vendors is primarily a problem of the pavement and roadside vendors. The problem arises because vendors spill over leading to overcrowding and congestion in the area. This problem becomes more acute in busy commercial areas particularly in areas having narrow lanes and by-lanes. Eviction of roadside vendors to clear them off the government or Municipal land and from the main roads are conducted from time to time. Often, it is observed that such operations help to temporarily clear the area but many vendors come back to the same location after a few days. An alternative could be to provide space in a side lane to the sellers with provision of clean water, electricity and garbage disposal. This is possible only if this essential service is legitimized.

Though the Guwahati Municipal Corporation tries to control street food vending by requiring licences, yet it is seen that obtaining of licence is a lengthy and a time consuming process and permission to occupy space is seldom granted. Thus, majority of vendors operate without a licence. All such vendors have to pay Rs. 5 daily as encroachment fee to the municipality, which is a good source of revenue, which no government would like to do away with. In addition, the cost of replacing either the food service or the employment would be beyond the means of most developing countries. Therefore, instead of following a policy of harassment and destruction on one hand and generating revenue from these petty traders on the other, the government should try and legitimize this important activity.

This study calls upon all concerned to recognise street food vending as a required urban amenity and not a nuisance to be removed for creating congestion and pollution problems. The following suggestions are offered which could help this informal yet vital service sector and also mitigate the problems:

(i) Legitimized space should be provided to the street food vendors in the high vending concentration areas; a little away from the main roads, preferably in a side road where customers can reach them. This will eliminate congestion.

(ii) The vendors should be registered for a specified time period and a fee charged for the space. This money should be directly utilised in the maintenance of spacc allottcd. Basic facilities like drinking water, garbage disposal, lighting, etc. should be provided.

(iii) There is a need for creation of "food parks" in select recreation centres where cleanliness and hygiene are strictly maintained.

(iv) Vendors should be made aware of the importance of hygiene. Regular inspection should be conducted.

(v) Organising vendor into associations would make administering of the vending spaces easier, also it would help in voicing vendor's grievances.

In conclusion, this study urges upon the government to legitimize this vital service and support it though proper planning and credit facilities so as to make street food vending healthy, convenient and desirable.

References

Bhattacharyya, Mini, 1997, " Street Food Vending in Urban Guwahati. An Anthropological Appraisal." Unpublished Ph.D. thesis. Gauhati University.

Tinker, Irene, 1987, "Street Foods : Testing Assumption about Informal Sector Activity by Women and Men." Entire Issues of Current Sociology 35/3.

Tinker, Irene (1997), *Street Foods, Urban Food and Employment in Developing Countries*, New York . Oxford Univ. Press.

19

CRIMES AGAINST WOMEN IN GREATER GUWAHATI

Polly Vauquline

Guwahati in the last twenty-five years has grown tremendously in all the sectors due to rapid urbanisation. In this process of urbanisation and modernisation there are witnesses of certain socio-cultural degradation by analysing the following aspects:

1. The various forms of crimes against women in Greater Guwahati.
2. The rate of growth of this crime.

In this paper, it is realised that the social status of women cannot be raised without eliminating the "Crime Against Women".

Crime Against Women in Greater Guwahati

Urbanisation is considered as an indicator of modernisation. In this process of urbanisation there are witnesses of socio-cultural degradation. One of the indicators of this socio-cultural environment degradation is the alarming rise of crimes in general and crimes against women in particular in Guwahati, the capital city of Assam and the Gateway of North East India.

Guwahati, one of the oldest urban centres of North East India is a fast growing metropolis. Greater Guwahati covers an area of 313 sq. km on both banks of the Brahmaputra river. A large part of the city is located on the crescent shaped plain lying on the southern bank of the Brahmaputra river in Kamrup district of Assam. The city has grown over 80 times since the beginning of the century when it was only 2.95 sq. km in 1900. During the last four decades, the population of the city has grown from 48,615 in 1951 to 100,707 in 1961 and again to 584,342 in 1991. The population has exploded nearly 5 times in last two decades from 123,783 in 1971 to 584,342 in 1991 (Table 19.1). This radical growth of population is primarily due to the rapid growth of professional institution, educational institution, cultural institution, commercial centres etc. Simultaneously, with the growth of people of different works of life, there co-existed the growth of crimes in the city, more so the crimes against women.

Table 19.1 : Population Characteristics of Guwahati

Year	Persons	Male	Female	% Variation
1901	11,661	7,772	3,889	–
1911	12,481	8,138	4,343	+7.03
1921	16,480	10,786	5,684	+32.04
1931	21,797	14,506	7,291	+32.26
1941	29,598	18,883	10,715	+35.79
1951	48,615	27,990	15,625	+47.36
1961	100,707	67,289	33,429	+130.90
1971	123,783	75,583	48,200	+22.19
1991	584,342	327,725	256,617	

Source : Census of India, 1991.

Women has been an important subject of study since the last few decades. A huge mass of literature on the history of women has already appeared in the Western languages. In India, as well, there have been a good number of studies conducted on women. In the contemporary India today the subject has received so much attention that it has virtually become a burning topic of discussion for the media and the people.

Guwahati is a masculine city. The sex ratio of the city has always been lower than the state's sex ratio (Table 19.2). It has the lowest sex ratio among the urban centres of Assam. It is one of the primary causes for rapid increase of crimes against women in the city. This alarming rise of crimes against women in the city calls for a serious speculation for the development of the society.

Table 19.2 : Decadal variation in Sex ratio of Population of Assam and Guwahati

Year	1901	1911	1921	1931	1941	1951	1961	1971	1981	1991
Assam	919	915	895	874	875	868	869	869	900	925
Guwahati	500	534	528	503	567	558	497	638	–	783

Source : Census of India, 1991.

Objective

In this paper an attempt has been made to study the crime against women in Greater Guwahati. The objective taken for this study are:

1. To highlight the various forms of crimes against women existing in Guwahati city.
2. To analyse the rate of this crime.
3. To suggest measures to put a check to the growth of this crime.

Data Base and Methodology

The Greater Guwahati covering an area of 313 sq. km. has been selected for this study. The city is bounded by 26°5` N to 26°12` N latitudes and 91°24` E to 91°51` E longitudes.

Crimes Against Women

The gender differences and bias perceived as existing globally, places women in the physical and psychological violence perpetuated on them. Notwithstanding the equality guaranteed through the constitution, many women's life is stalked by various threats of violence. The threat of violence on women manifests right before their life begins, continues to scar their early life, follows in the married life as domestic violence, endangers as victims of rapes and worse than that ends in murders or suicide in some cases. In the recent United Nations Development Plan Report it has been stated that "even under law, the equality of women is not yet assured in many societies let alone in practise". It further adds "Although violence stalks women lives, laws can do little unless present cultural and social values changes". In this context the issue of crime and violence against women is a serious social concern.

In India, the Constitution and several legislations guarantee women equality, freedom, opportunity and protection. Nonetheless, they continue to be victims of domestic violence, family violence, violence in the community and at work places.

The concern for one of this major problem amply justifies isolating all identified crimes, wherein women alone are victims as "Crime Against Women". Although women may be victims in any of the crime, be it 'murder', 'robbery', 'cheating' or any other, the crimes in which women are victims and which is directed specially against women are characterised as 'Crimes Against Women'.

Crimes against women are broadly classified under two categories.

1. *The crimes identified under the Indian Panel Code (IPC)*:
   - (i) Rape (376 IPC)
   - (ii) Kidnapping and Abduction for different purposes (363-373 IPC)
   - (iii) Homicides for Dowry, Dowry Death or their attempts (302-304 IPC)
   - (iv) Torture, both mental and physical (498A IPC)
   - (v) Molestation (354 IPC)
   - (vi) Sexual harassment (509 IPC)
   - (vii) Importation of girls (upto 21 yrs. of age) (366-B IPC)

2. *The crimes identified under the Special Laws (SLL)*:

Reprehensible social practices such as commission of sati, demand for dowry, trafficking of women for immoral purposes etc. are identified as offences punishable under the following .social enactments to safeguard women and their interest, specially. They are :

(i) Commission of Sati (Prevention) Act, 1956.
(ii) Dowry Prohibition Act, 1961.
(iii) Immoral Traffic (Prevention) Act, 1956.
(iv) Indecent Representation of Women Prohibition Act, 1986.

Crimes Against Women in Guwahati

In All-India crime rate for the recorded crimes against women during 1995 was 11.6. Based on the crime rate at national levels, sates/ union territory, have been categorised as 'more crime prone' and 'less crime prone' areas for crimes that are perpetrated against women (Table 19.3).

Table 19.3 : Incidence and rate of crimes committed against women in Assam, 1992-95

Year	Incidence	% Contribution to All India Total	Estimated Mid-Year Population (in Lakhs)	Rate	Rank
1992	1520	1.9	230.8	66	21
1993	–	–	–	–	–
1994	1545	1.6	241.1	6.4	23
1995	2831	2.7	246.1	11.5	10

The rate of crimes against women in Assam has shown a significant rise in the last few years. It was 6.6 in 1992 and has gone upto 11.5 in 1995 and so has the All India rank in the rate of crimes committed against women. In 1995 its rank was 10th whereas in 1992 it was 21st .

From the data collected from different police stations of Greater Guwahati and the City S. P. Office, Guwahati, it has been found out that there has been a steady growth of crimes against women in the city since 1980. Even though the number of crimes committed under each head for each year could not be obtained, the rate of crime in this last two decades shows a upward trend. The number of incidences has increased from 43 in 1980 to 239 in 1998 (Table 19.4). There is nearly a six fold increase in the rate of crimes against women in the last 19 years.

Table 19.4 : Incidence and rate of crimes committed against women in Guwahati, 1980-98

Year	Kidnapping	Molestation	Rape	Burnt Alive	Dowry death	Atrocities	Murder	Eve Teasing	Total
1980	24	13	6	–	–	–	–	–	43
1981	29	19	1	–	–	–	–	–	49
1982	25	19	8	–	–	1	–	2	55
1983	31	27	9	–	–	1	–	–	68
1984	30	31	13	–	–	–	–	1	75
1985	29	10	13	2	–	2	–	2	58
1986	50	30	14	2	–	2	–	1	99
1987	33	29	13	6	1	16	4	7	109
1988	34	31	16	1	1	13	6	20	122
1989	63	34	39	5	1	35	2	21	200
1990	84	36	33	–	–	17	1	2	173
1991	93	52	28	–	1	15	2	9	200
1992	71	51	25	–	2	20	2	2	173
1993	69	43	29	–	–	21	5	3	168
1994	66	55	29	–	1	36	1	5	193
1995	68	60	39	–	–	38	–	–	205
1996	68	66	26	–	1	36	16	–	211
1997	81	39	25	–	2	55	4	–	206
1998	108	42	36	–	8	38	7	–	239

The registration of kidnapping cases is more in Jalukbari, Panbazar, Paltanbazar and in Chandmari police station. It is mostly from the Assamese family.

Cases lodged against Dowry death is more from the Hindu Bengali and Marwari dominated areas, such as Paltanbazar,

Jalukbari and Fatasil police station. But in the last few years a number of cases are reported in the other police stations from people belonging to other communities also. Dowry death cases are very rare in Assamese family.

The number of cases registered against molestation is high in Dispur and Paltanbazar police station. They are mostly registered by women belonging to lower castes or who are of lower economic group.

Molestation cases are generally suppressed when it occurs in high class qualified family.

The registration of rape cases are almost similar in all the police stations.

It is quite interesting to note that the cases of atrocities against women is more in the newly settled areas and in the extension areas of Greater Guwahati.

The above stated informations were critically analysed and was shared by the concerned persons engaged in maintaining the statistical records of Crime Against Women of Greater Guwahati of City S. P. Office, Guwahati. They also highlighted that the number of crimes against women are high in those areas of the city which are thickly populated.

Concluding Observation

It is well documented fact that there is a gradual growth of number of crimes committed against women in Greater Guwahati. It calls for serious speculation and critical examination. The concern for one of this major problem amply justifies isolating, all identified crimes where in women alone are victims as "Crime Against Women" and tackle the same with utmost expedience. By strengthening women's role in providing equal opportunity and share in the fruits of developments only the status of women can be raised. Any measure to eliminate violence against women without raising their social status and life without equality as enshrined in Universal Declaration of Human Rights, would hardly facilitate any further reduction in the crime against women.

References

Ananthachari, T., " Violence Against Womcn", The *Assam Tribune*, March 8, 1998.

Atray, J.P., *Crimes Against Women*, Published by Vikas Publishing House Pvt. Ltd., New delhi, 1988, pp. 8-13.

Census of India, 1991, Director of Census Operation, Assam.

Crimes in India, Published by National Crime Record Bureau, 1995, New Delhi.

Sahai, S.N., *Women in Changing Society*, Published by Mittal Publication, New Delhi, 1985, pp. 15-16.

20

CHANGE OF VALUES AS REFLECTED IN CULTURE AND LITERATURE

Taranee Deka

The statistics show that the process of urbanisation in Assam is very slow. According to Census Report, 1961 there are only 60 towns in Assam and the number of industries is very few. Guwahati was recognised as a city only in 1971. At present Assam has four towns with population more than one lac. The rate of industrialisation is very slow. We have only some industries belonging to service sectors, not primary or secondary. In Kamrup District the total number of registered industries are 275 in 1996, all of them are either small scale or medium scale units. Upto June 1999, there are only three large scale units, namely Kamakhya Cements, N.E. Pure Drinks and Pioneer Cryogenic in the private sector and Guwahati Refinery in the public sector. The big capitalists outside the state are not willing to invest in Assam for the extremist problem. In the 80s a good number of industries like steel units, asbestos etc. started to grow along N.H.No. 31 from Amingaon to Changsari. More than thousand units got registered. But, due to stepped-up militant activities, these units were closed one after another. Under such political and economic condition, one cannot expect to grow a fully city culture without the growth of capitalism. The rural-urban differences are almost nil in the developed countries like U.K. or U.S.A. The agriculture sector is also mechanised there. So, we have a century-old town civilization by the big capitals with the associations of an educated, skilled working class scattered in cities and villages. In Assam, the city life, even hasn't been modernised like Calcutta, Delhi or Mumbai. Not in the big industries, a group of youths are coming to open small units like tea plantation in small scale or a plastic, candle or aluminium products. So, a city culture is starting to grow in Assam and in Guwahati it is gaining momentum day by day. Though, Guwahati is a full city as defined by census report, in the mental horizon of the city it is one kind of induced urban settlement. Some traditional values are still in practice. The opening of Saraighat bridge, the expansion of broad gauge railway line in 80s the newly introduced trains connecting all the major cities of India, the expansion of Borjhar air port (now Gopinath Bordoloi International Airport) and air services to all cities, the establishments of N.E. Offices, state offices of Government Semi-Government. and private companies, the establishment of Guwahati IIT, the expansion of management and computer education through NERIM, NEIBM, NIIT etc., the availability of informations through INTERNET, E-Mail, speedpost, the improved tele-communications, the establishments of many new degree colleges, the modern nursing homes with world-class facilities, the expanding city bus services both in public and private sectors, the expansion of English education in the private sectors, the opening of T.V. centre at Guwahati and the introduction of Cable T.V. services, the increased number of books, newspapers, magazines, the starting of some new markets at Ganeshguri, Paltanbazar, Beltola, Noonmati, Jalukbari, Adabari, the revolution in the road transport system by Blue Hill, Green Valley, Network etc. are important factors that has changed the face of Guwahati beyond recognition after 1972. With the expansion of Guwahati many new people have here some for services in Central Government services and company jobs, others for permanent settlement. The new settlers, mostly from the Lower Assam have settled in the peripheral area. So, there is a difference of mentality between the people of old town area or central Guwahati and the new area in the periphery of the city. Now, all the five lacs plus people of Guwahati have been living in the city for many years. With the passing of time, one can notice the changes in their culture like in family organisation, marriage, foods etc. The new situations have brought in new values like critical appreciating power, open-mindedness, tale for music and other fine arts and awareness in politics etc. On the other hand like other city people it has made the Guwahatians more individualistic, more selfish, alienated from community life etc. These changes in values can be observed in literature also, particularly in the fictions.

Cultural Change

Many urban studies show that cities in India continue to be dominated by cultural and structural attributes which are far different from those which are considered to be typical for a city, *e.g.* formalisation, atomisation, lack of familialsm and kin-bound groupings and predominance of secular ideologies etc. Studies reveal on the other hand, that in the Indian context a rural-urban dichotomy is untidy, if not irrelevant, contrary to the stereo-type, familistic norms and joint family structures have been found, the neighbourhood pattern and some cities studied is organised on caste and kinship lines similar to the villages, the migratory pattern in the city is also closely related with ties of kinship and acquaintance. Urbanisation is a process without breakdown in the traditional pattern. In Assam this is true. We have a twin culture of rural and urban values blended together. So, we have physical development of city like Guwahati in Assam, but mentally it has not reached the state of urbanism. After 1972, Guwahati has become the nerve-centre of N.E. India. Now let us examine the changes in various fields.

Family Organisation

In the central and peripheral areas of Guwahati most of the settlers have the professions of Government. and non-Government services. They are educated and are bound by economic scarcity.

This group is the arch member of the influential middle class. The other people living in the city area are also educated. Under the city condition they show some changes in the family organisation. A study on "Urbanisation and social change" (1990) in the Anthropology department, Gauhati University by R.Hazarika finds the fact that the joint family system, which is an expression of community life is on the wane. After that about eight years have passed and that too under the impact of new economic policy, i.e. GATT Treaty and many other powerful factors of globalisation. In the study out of 1902 families surveyed belonging to various classes of people and scattering central and peripheral areas, the number of nuclear family was 1650, horizontal joints 192, vertical joints 90 and horizontal-cum-vertical joints 60. The survey of Census report, 1971 also reveals the fact that nuclear type of families are the most common one in Guwahati. It is pertinent here that in the urban situation most of the vertical joint families exist temporarily only, because the sons after marriage form a nuclear family independenty bearing their parents. So, the one of nuclear families claims to be the highest nuclear, which is an urban trend. In the central area, some joint families, particularly horizontal joint (Brother + Brother) can be seen till date. It is became partly it is an age-old continuity of community life and partly because they cannot afford to live separately due to scarcity of land. As to the size of the family the percentage of small family (1-3 member) being 29.58 and medium size family (4-6 member) being 62.42 and combined total is 92% which substantiates the first observation of nuclear type family. The small families maintain kinship visiting their relations in holidays or at the time of family festival. So, they maintained both individualism and traditionalism in this respect. In the 90s, the only one-child concept has gained much popularity among the service-holders due to increasing expenses. Except few community, almost everybody has taken the measure of birth control. The educated persons know to take care of thier children following scientific measures. This generation of children, who have received all facilities and care tend to be more individualistic.

Marriage

In the traditional Assamese marriages, all the family members heartily participate and extends help from inviting people to the sharing of expenditures as defined. The community participation is an indication of community life. But in the 80s and 90s it is not so. With the change of time, even the peripheral area like Japarigog, Jatiya, Khanapara, Azara etc. have witnessed changes in the choices of bride or grooms or arrangement of marriages. Assamese people don't prefer inter-caste and inter-community marriages. It has been proved by the said study on "Urbanisation and Social Change" (1990). In the study, it was found that Assamese males preferred to marry Assamese girls. Out of the surveyed couples, the percentage of males being 99.62% and females being 99.4% only 38% males and 6% females have married non-Assamese counterparts. (That is why, the assimilation in Assamese society could not complete). But in the 90s the percentage will be more. But in other aspects, the changes are remarkable. As to love-marriages, inter-caste marriages, divorce etc., the city people are departing from the traditional values. This has been proved right by another study by education department, G.U. in 1978. The interviewed girls were grouped into two groups, the first group of the age-group 22 to 27 and the second being of 16 to 22 age-group. The selected girls were from G.U., Cotton College and Handique Girls' College, Guwahati. The findings are as follows:

(i) Love-marrriage	Yes–48%	(Group-I)	No–52%
	57%	(Group-II)	63%
(ii) Inter-caste-marriage	Yes–64%	(Group-I)	No–36%
	71%	(Group-II)	29%
(iii) Court-marriage	Yes–30%	(Group-I)	No–70%
	40%	(Group-II)	60%
(iv) Divorce due to regular or permanent conflict	Yes–62%	(Group-I)	No–38%
	72%	(Group-II)	28%
(v) Marriages during study	Yes–20%	(Group-I)	No–80%
	65%	(Group-II)	35%

In the 90s the response for 'yes' will be more. Because girls are more educated and they are more concerned about women's rights. All the five categories of questions put to the girls in the study were dominated by traditional 'No' till 60s. Now, divorce or inter-caste or court-marriage is not a difficult job for women. In 1997, Nalini Singh in her popular serial '*Hello India*' interviewed some ten girls at Guwahati as to their opinions on women's rights. Some of them even supported the extra marital relationships. These new views on marriages by Assamese women are the results of expansion of education as a modernising factor. Apart from these, some changes are observed in the celebration of marriages. The tent houses have taken the places of community in the smooth organisation of marriages. The marriage places are decorated heavily, even rich people bring internal decorators from outside the state. It has, in fact, become a status symbol. The buffer system has abolished the idea of community feast. The food items were distributed by deputed persons from community till 70s. The video-recording of the marriage-ceremony is a new thing in marriage what was not possible earlier.

Dresses and Foods

Traditional Assamese dresses are seen only in the festivals, that too women's dresses like Mekhela Chadar or Pat dresses. The textile advertisements through Hindi and Holywood cinemas and T.V. programmes and the growth and development of fashion and beauty as a technology new dresses are coming everyday. The market economy also are helping in the introduction of new dresses. The establishments of big textile mills in the country and the showrooms at Guwahati like Goenka Readymades, Goenka Sari House, Sarmah Beach Fashion etc. have also contributed towards the popularisation of new and non-traditional dresses. Even people liked the Park-Avenues, Hoffman, Newport, Blue Lagoon brand of favourite dresses. The casual dresses like genes and T-Shirts have become very popular among the youths. The recent studies show, that even the tribal people like Karbis of Bholukchuk, Bodo-Kacharis of Kachari-Basti, Ravas of Jatia have been influenced by modern fashions. Now, they even put on (except the old people) pants, shirts, coats of western types modern sweaters etc. Chadar-Kamij has become a common dress among the girls. Even married women are robed in such dresses instead of traditional Sari or Mekhela Chadar. The girls even put on genes, pants, shirts, tops and tiny gowns. In the name of fashion and comfort our traditional dresses have been given up. All are robed in borrowed dresses—the traditional dresses can be seen only in marriage party or festivals, even the traditional dresses like Mekhela Chadar and Pat dresses have been influenced by modern design and print.

With the modernisation of some values the foodhabit of the Assamese people particularly at Guwahati have also been changing, adding new food items to the menu. The Assamese uses varieties of food-items as breakfast, dinner or tiffin. Nowhere in India one will get so many varieties of food like in Assam. With the changing time as city people are turning professionals and highly time-conscious, they cannot prepare varieties of food-items. Moreover, the women are also not like the traditional housewives. They are also busy in service or in business. So, they have turned to fast-food. A traditional food like Ghillapitha (one kind of rice cake), Chungapitha etc. are made of rice-powder involving lot of time and labour. The modern food technology and the food-processing big companies also tempt people to change their food-habits. As for example, the use of Ghee (purified butter) has increasingly been replaced by vegetable oil, not only in Guwahati, but also in the other rural places of Assam. Prof. S.N. Srinivas writes about the Mysore region this way—"*that popularity of travel and tea shops is not confined to city folk but extends to villages as well*". After the expansion of Guwahati it has become a cosmopolitan city, officers and executives, workers and businessmen are coming to the city to work. They want to take foods of their own culture. The rising Assamese middle class also want to take various foods for the said reasons. To cater the needs of these people a number of new hotels and restaurants has sprang up here and there, serving their customers South Indian dishes, Chinese dishes, Continental dishes and North Indian dishes. In the early 70s, 'Dosa and 'Idli' were found only in Malabar Hotel at Panbazar. Now, it is found even in a temporary foot-path tea-shops. In rural area also, the hotels and teashops have popularised many food items. Many three and four star hotels like the Hotel Brahmaputra, Ashoka, the Belliview, the Prag Continental, the Dynasty, Kuber International and modern restaurants like Woodland, Picadilly, Sanflower etc. are providing food items what one can get at any places of India. The new soft drinks Thumps-up, Pepsi, Cocacola, Mirinda etc., the packeted fast food items like Chou (Noodles), Chewei, Uncle Chips, Kellog's Cornflakes, preserved tin meat, Sea-fish, Pork, Paneer etc., the solid foods like momo, mushroom, cutlets etc. are becoming extremely popular not only in the said class of people, even the peripheral areas have been influenced by these foods. Among the tribal people of Japarigog, Jatia, Kacharibasti and the Ninemiles, tea has become a common food instead of traditional, home-made drinks. The new brands of foreign liquors are available in the city. With the opening of hundreds of wineshops, wine has become very popular, thereby bellying the common talk that those, who take wine are drunkards. People have accepted it in general.

Language

Language also goes on changing with the passage of time. The present Assamese language is not the same what it was in the days of Sankardeva. Since the beginning of the Assamese language many morphological, semantic and phonological changes have taken place. It is true with the language of the Guwahatians also. The language what they speak now is not chaste Assamese. It in neither the dialect of Upper Assam or of Kamrup. As educated persons, they try to use the written form of the language and both the said dialects have influenced each other and thereby it turned into a mix language. Most of the new migrants in the peripheral area are from the Lower Assam districts, where Kamrupi dialect in much used. But, like other changes, they use the written form. But in town it is not so. Sometimes the Guwahati language flouts the grammatical rules also. As for example, the boys and girls of present day Guwahati use "*Moi gharat jaba lage*" which should be "*moi gharaloi jaba lage*". Again, "*Moi bhat khai kene collegot jam*", which should be "*Moi bhat khai uthi College.....*" or "*Moi bhat khai uthar pichat....*", "*Khai hol Ne?*" instead of "*Khowa hol Ne?*" The words used in the Uzanbazar area also different, they use slang words like 'Be', 'Kela', etc. In the stylistic form of the language, most of the Guwahatians had the general tendency to use English words in Assamese sentence, which is known as "Code-mixing" in sociolinguistics. Codeswitching is also another style where they use English sentences in Assamese conversation. The latter has been popular in the 90s. In the celebration of traditional Bihu festivals, the entry of the big companies is a new thing. Now, the big-budgeted Bihu festivals at Latasil, Chandmari, Bharalumukh etc. are sponsored by big companies. Apart from Bihu songs, other modern songs are also presented in the cultural nites of the festival. The Bihu stage is also used by the music companies for publicity of new albums. This commercialisation of the festival is a new thing in the greater Guwahati. In the field of music also, the use of key-board, drum-sets, Sexophone, kongo etc. has made the Assamese modern song a different one. A new group of singers like Jitul Sonowal, Jubin Garg, Kumar Bhabesh, Mahalaksmi have blended western music with the traditional songs. A group of new film makers like Dr. Bhabendra Nath Saikia, Jahnu Barua, Sanjib Hazarika and Santana Bordoloi are providing new taste to the city middle class people with new ideas.

Assamese Culture and Cultural Imperialism

There is a correlation between the new cultural values (positive or negative) and the cultural market. After the demise of erstwhile Soviet Union, the world's big capital under the leadership of USA has been dominating the international politics and market since 90s. The third world countries of Asia, Africa and Latin America are the target area for U.S. big capitals to sell their cultural products. In the beginning of this paper, it is mentioned that the urbanisation in Assam is only in physical side, but mentally they have not been able to build up a true urban culture. So, baring a small percentage of people, the changes for the general masses are the result of blind imitation or snobery. The atmosphere and social conditions of the western countries are different from us. So, their values cannot be repeated here *in toto*. There is a constant threat from US-backed cultural imperialism to the diversity of culture. The spirit of individualism and mono-culture are encouraged to break the traditional community life with multi-faceted cultures. Ayn Rand, a noted thinker of the contemporary US culture and literature has been propagating the theory of individualism and denouncing the welfare state concept since the 60s through her novels, drama and critical writings. To quote her, "*...Ethics is not a mystic fantasy nor a social convention—nor a dispensable, subjective luxury,......Ethics is an objective necessity of man's survival—not by the grace of the supernatural nor of your neighbours nor of your whims, but by the grace of reality and the nature of life........The objective ethics proudly advocates and upholds rational selfishness—which means : the values required for human survival—not the values produced by the desires, the feelings, the whims or the needs of irrational brutes, who have never outglore the primordial practice of human sacrifices*". This rational selfishness forms the basis of capitalistic ideas. Some may be benefited personally by such selfish nature, but it is a great blow to the age-old community life. The impact of Hollywood's cinemas of sex and violence, the Hindi pictures of the same taste, the twenty-four hours Cable T.V. programmes have led the young generation to the loss of sensibility—an indispensable quality for humanism. It is seen in the murder of Gautam Barua by his class-mates in Cotton College, the killing practice for money by some youths at Guwahati. The cases of Eve-teasing, dacoities, rape have increased alarmingly at Guwahati. The traditional values like fellow-feeling, friendship, love, humanity etc. are on the wane. The new values replacing the old values are motivated and based on self-interest only. The inhuman-killings and kidnapping in the name of revolution by some militant outfit has also contributed towards this state of affairs. In such situation, common people are at cross-roads perplexed at the development. According to Edward Said, eminent writer, has said that the print media in USA has been polluting the newspapers with news-items. The press barons select the news-items for printing in the world news-paper through news agencies. People in USA are also not informed about some incidents. They are also trying to replace 'book' with news-paper's literary supplements. In the news-papers of Guwahati also this can be observed. This way the Guwahatians are at cross-roads—they are maintaining a dual culture—the one, going weaker day by day and the other, yet to consolidate its position. It will take, perhaps, some more years to have a complete urban culture by the people of Guwahati.

Change in Literature

Behind every book there is an author and behind every author there is an age and a society. However, great or small a writer may be he is not an isolated being. The writers of Assamese literature have also been living through the changes of society. After the expansion of Guwahati, they have gathered new experiences by meeting people, by travelling and by reading books. Many authors have settled in Guwahati. The new values for urbanisation like critical mind, open-mind, secular spirit have craved in their minds and they begin to observe the things from a different point view, what was not there before 70s. The urban services and science and technology brought to them a ray of hope, on the other hand the endless migration, the increased population, the poverty, the slums, the juvenile crimes and all other problems of a city settlement made them frustrated and cynic. The acute inflation rate, the unemployment problem, the political unrest of the whole N.E. region and the other related problems have added fuel to the fire. They are creating a situation of hopelessness and void among the youths right from the 80s. Only a small section of the city citizens are happy with the development. It is true many youths have come forward to open business and some have' services in Government or Semi-Government department also. In such a critical and pathetic situation a group of writers, particularly the fiction writers have responded to it and have reflected the situation in their works. The breakdown of rural England and the emergence of Industrial England is the theme of the 'wessex novels' by Thomas Hardy. In the novels of Charles Dickens, we have a very good picture of industrial England

and its people. Joul Paul Satre Simon De Bourir, Franj Kafha, Milan Kundera, Gabriel Marquiz etc. have recreated this new world in the context of their own land. The heartless people of London and Hollowness of modern civilization were best expressed by Wordsworth and T.S. Eliot in their poems :

...The wealthiest among us is the best;
No grandeur now in nature or in book
Delights us, Rapine, avarice, expense.
This is idolatry; and these we adore;
Plain living and high thinking no more.

(Wordsworth, Sonnet, London, September-1802)

Eliot is upset with this state of hollowness that he did not see a single person with humanity, a son of the soil, among the crowd across the London bridge in the misty October month. They are, according to him, lifeless, ghosts in the Danfe's hell—

So many
I had not thought death had undone
So many,

(T.S. Eliot, Wateland)

'Guwahati' is praised in the description of a poem published in Orunodoi in 1846. But those days of peace are gone. Now, the reality is different. In the 90s apart from other problems, it has become safe place and hide-outs for the militants. The change of values and atmosphere of Guwahati have become the subjects for writing. Some fiction writers, particularly Sourav Kumar Chaliha, Devabrat Das, Manoj Kumar Goswami, etc. in short stories and Homen Borgohain, Debabrata Das, Nabin Barua, Phanindra Kumar Dev Choudhury, Bhupendra Narayan Bhattacharya etc. in novels have drawn a picture of urban life, which are discussed below in a nutshell.

Sourav Kumar Chaliha made a remarkable departure from the traditional short story both in content and form with the publication of " Ashanta Electron" this change was noticed in Assamese Short Stories. He was followed by Debabrata Das in the 70s. Let us first see the change in subject-matter. In short stories of Sourav Kumar Chaliha after the 70s, the subject of 'Bina Kutir' is about an old home. The house stands for the traditional values. It is now a bone of contention between the two brothers as inheritors. The elder one is a professor, busy in textbook and notesbook writing. He wants to open a press there, because if he publishes the books from his press the profit will increase. The younger one is a doctor, he wants to build an R.C.C. home there making one room as his Chamber on the ground-floor. So, symbolically the traditional values are standing among the attacking capitalist values. Another story *Bhraman Birati* (Interlude in travelling) is about the life-struggle in a heartless world. Here, the struggle for livelihood turns into death wishes. The description of a heartless city, Calcutta full of sounds and uncertainty. In spite of its unpleasant nature he moves to this city. Because his beloved lives in this city. So there is a contradiction in the mind, he hates the city, yet he comes for his beloved. Similarly, in first short story collection of Debabrata Das called *Arpitar Erati* (The one night of Arpita) published in 1978. Being born and brought up in Guwahati and an engineering graduate Sri Das has choosen very modern subjects as the theme of his stories. The urban problems like poverty, prostitution, films of Mrinal Sen, the mystic and silent beauty of a girl in a train journey, the Naxalbari movement, new art-films and art exhibitions etc. are the subjects for Sri Das' short stories, which are very new in Assamese short story. The way how the author or his characters responded to these subjects are the expressions of the changed values due to urbanisation. Definitely, the new middle class of the Assamese society settled at Guwahati has come out as a distinct class with different tastes and a cultured mind. Let us see the subjects of Sri Das in Arpitar Erati. In one story called *Behur Bahirot Abhimanyu* (Abhimanyu outside the....). The story centres round an unemployed educated youth of Guwahati. Abhimanyu, was looking for jobs years after years. The name of the story itself suggests that it is a new interpretation of the story in the *Mahabharata*. His elder sister is running the family somehow working in a Marowari Farm. She has been exploited physically there, but she cannot give up the job. She arrived late at night indicating her gradual involvement in the line of a fallen women. One day, Abhimanyu discovers to his utter surprise that his sister has become pregnant. She has no extra money for having an abortion, a fees of Rs. five hundred. But she must be saved of this ignominy and she should remain fit for maintaining the family till his employment elsewhere. So, he starts pick-pocketing in the city bus, public places. In one of his attempts he was caught redhanded and the story ends with the people chasing him. The ending of the story is quite unusual as because instead of fleeing away Abhimanyu stops to run and questions his followers whether they are themselves thief or not involving in corruption or others. The description of prostitution and the meek acceptance of this fact by her family members are new things in the story—which is a bi-product of urbanisation. The story 'Arpitar Erati', I think is one of the best stories in Assamese Literature. The protagonist is travelling with a girl in a train. She is accompanied by (perhaps) her father. Right from the beginning the narrator in first person was observing the girl—who was putting on a beautiful face with the colour of natural tenderness and sadness. He was busy analysing the reasons behind her sadness and enjoying the silent beauty also. At night, when everybody in that compartment was sleeping she was weeping. At one time she went to the door and was about to jump. The protagonist saved her from her peril. This type of subject was quite new in late 70s. The author has taetfully used the guilty feeling of the protagonist in the story. The story of the girl, her attempt to suicide and subsequent rescue etc. are the projection of the protagonist's mind, who was once a revolutionary. He wanted to fight with corruption, misrule and wanted to drive away poverty from this world. But, in course of time, he found a very safe and comfortable life in a Government Service, and got fascinated with the middle class life. So he wanted to get rid of his guilty feelings deep rooted in the sub-conscious mind and ultimately found an outlet in the rescue story of Arpita. The well-knit story is fully of psycho-analysis and like ghost-story the suspense is well-maintained till end.

Another short-story writer, Manoj Kumar Goswami has been trying to bring new subjects in his stories. With his debut publication, namely 'Samiran Baura Ahi Ache' (Samiran Barua is coming) in 90s he dealt with yet other themes like the extremist problem, the secret world of middle class people, unemployment problem etc. in his stories. Even the impact of the fall of the erstwhile Soviet Union on one communist is the subject of one of his stories. In the story 'Samiran Barua Ahi Ache' we find an extremist leader, who is returning to his native town after many years' of vigorous training in Kochin. His arrival to the town is a matter of discussion for all kinds of people including his beloved, police and others. The story develops with the reactions of the people regarding Samiran Barua. He found that his people for whom he has been in a very strenuous training, has given up his youth – was not changing at all. He did not feel to meet anybody, even his beloved. He came and returned the same way disgusting at the people's mentality. So he purchased some cashews and was eating to pass-time. The story 'Tala' (the lock) is about the secrets of middle class life. The wife discovered (after her husband's sudden death) in the personal box that many things were unknown to her in spite of their long conjugal life. People have some secrets that cannot be discovered, they are purely personal. In 'Godessness' (like 'thoughtlessness' of Sourav Kumar Chaliha) one unemployed youth has prayed for death of one person so that he might be recruited in that vacancy. These are quite new subjects in Assamese short story. As mentioned earlier, some other story writers also wrote stories on new topics.

The other genere of literature that expresses the urban values well in novels. In the Victorian age, after the Industrial revolution the new age and values were expressed in the form of novels. The complexities of the industrial life were best revealed in novels only. That is why English literature, during that period was flooded with novels. In Assamese literature also, Guwahati after its expansion and modernisation became the breeding place for novels. A host of writers like Homen Borgohain, Debabrata Das, Dr. Dhrubajyoti Bora, Nabin Barua, Phanindra Kumar Dev Choudhury, Polen Borkataki, Dilip Dutta, Bhupen Sarma, Basanta Das, Parag Kumar Das and many others started to write novels with new themes, characters and form in order to express the changing situation and to provide taste to the new urban middle class. It is worthy to mention that the increasing number of new magazines and news-papers acted as host to these writers Sadin, Budhbar, Asom Bani, Dainik Asom, Ranghar etc. took the leadrole in this respect. Let us find out some subjects of the new novels. Debabrata Das, like his short-stories has written many short novels. In one of his novels called "Bhanurator Din Rati" (The brokenable Day and Night) Sri Das used "The visit of Ajijul Haque to Guwahati and his public meeting". Haque is a famous navalite leader and he has been in jail from 1969 to recent times. In the 90s he visited Guwahati. The novelist has included one of his famous speeches, "I know, I have every right of my country's air, land, forest, rivers, winds etc. Delhi has been involved in a very cruel conspiracy to snatch away these rights from the people. I shall continue to support those, who oppose this heinous move". This is a very recent political topic and the author has critically examined it through his characters. Phanindra Dev Choudhury, known for "Anuradhar Desh", has in his novel, "Captive ULFA in the Fantacy Camera" exploited a very recent and burning problem of Assam. The author has established himself as an neutral observer while passing comments on the extremist outfit through various characters. Nabin Barua is famous for the novel "Cotton College" written in the 60s. In 'Smriti Hoba Khoja Suti Eta' (A rivulet willing to become a memory). We are shown the differences of outlooks, opinions, tastes etc. between two generations – the parents and their wards. Riti, who is the daughter of the narrator of the story, is living together with an artist at Delhi. They do not want to get married. Riti writes to her father that she does not want to disturb her boy-friend in his work by getting into wedlock. He has a dream and many things to do. Let him finish his work first. Marriage is a simple thing. On the other hand, Ritu, Karabi's daughter has joined in a militant organisation after passing Electronic Engineering shocking everybody. The narrator and his ex-beloved Karabi is discussing the problems of their wards at Duliajan Oil Township. The narrator confess, "We have not recognised this new generation. We also saw dreams, but we had no courage to break the tradition. They have been able to come out breaking the wall of traditional values – I do not know what is true, true will prove their values – we are meeck audiences only." The author has open mindedly criticised both the traditional and modern values. Though he has become emotional sometimes, his observation is neutral and balanced – an urban values. Dr. Dhrubajyoti Bora has brought a very new tropic in his novel "Phaenix" – the story about a drug-addicted and his subsequent giving up of the bad habit. The author as an social interventionist of the major social problems, linked the world of alienated drug-addict with the world of social movement. Both modern and traditional ideas have been posed one against other for comparison. This is the first novel written in the early nineties on such modern topic. Homen Borgohain's "Astarag" written in the 80s is a new kind of novel. The novel is based on "Old age". The responses of different characters to old age have been knitted in the theme. The hero, Dilip has a philosophical discussion on the topic with his friends. Moreover, his childhood experiences in rural set-up have also been described in flashback. The characters like Kaliram Pandit, Dilip's father etc. are the bearers of traditional values. Dilip, a lecturer of English literature, cherishes both the values. His response to different situations is objective and critical. It is based on the French novels of naturalism. Phanindra Deva Choudhury, like the already discussed novel on ULFA, has written other two novels on modern topics. In "Satyanusadhan" (Search for truth) he has delivered the mental world of a woman, who has lost one of her breast. It is story of nacked reality like one looking at one's own nacked image. The other one is "The mystery of death" – experiences of a old man who has witnessed so many deaths of his own sons and others. The novels are full of new images also. Most of the characters of the said novels are guided by the principle of individualism except a few like Dilip of Astarag.

Modern Assamese literature was begun with the spirit of humanism. Lakshminath Bezbarua, Chandrakumar Agarwala and Hemchandra Goswami exported this from western literature through "Jonaki". It continued for many years and even today we have residue of that spirit. But the demand of the age was different and promoted individualistic thought instead of social thought. The changes in content is accompanied by changes in form also. Sourav Kumar Chaliha is the torch bearer in giving up the traditional narrative style. Others following him came away from formal form and well-constructed plot. They have knitted the story like photographic film picking up different experiences and making a unity among them. The writers we have discussed above, in the line of Kafka, Borhes,

Milan Kundera, Gabriel Marquiza attempted their works. The socio-economic changes and the expansion of urban area and services are the main reasons behind this change. They tried to use flash-back technique in the time sequences. They have also used 'stream of consciousness' technique extensively. To represent an incident or situation, sometimes some poetical images have been used. We have for examples of new images used to express the same. (1) My poems are controlled by Boyle's Law, do you know Swati? (The Unfinished Story, Arpitar Erati, Debabrata Das). (2) Inside all men there is a video camera. I've recorded that particular moment for ever, off and on I play on that cassette, rewind, Replay... In the monitor of the mind one can see a tender hand first, like wave that hand comes through the crowd, touching me it leaves behind few precious moments.... after that in the monitor the actor's face is reflected. [Amabaisyar Andhakar Prithibit Jonak – (Moonlight in the dark World of Amabaisya) Phanindra Kumar Dev Choudhury]. A lot of examples can be cited new images. The language used in the short story or novels is also sophistical, polished and long sentences and complex sentences are used. In some case it is very poetic. These changes in form was the result of the social changes due to urbanisation. In this paper, only the good changes have been recorded for the fictional changes. It is also pertinent that sometimes these changes in literature was the blind imitation of foreign writers. So, in spite of the new form and content some piece of work could not succeed as all excellent pieces of art-work.

References

Datta Ray, B. , Dr. A.K. Neog, A.K.Hazhari, *Urbanisation in North East India: Problems and Potentiality* (ed.) Reliance Publishing House, New Delhi, 1998.

Ishwaran, K., *Urban Sociology* (ed.) Asia Publishing House, Bombay, 1965.

Mumford, Louis, *The Culture of Cities*, H&B Company, New York, 1938.

Rand, Ayn, *The Virtue of Selfishness*, Signet Books, Chicago, 1964.

Said, Edward, *Cultural Imperialism*, Vintage Books.

Singh, Yogendra, *The Modernisation of Indian Culture*, Rawat Publications, Jaipur, 1986.

Srinivas, S.N., *Social Change in Modern India*.

Turner, Roy, *India's Urban Future*, (ed.) University of California Press, 1962.

Asomiya Books and Journals :

১। সাহিত্যৰ সত্য, ড০ হীৰেণ গোহাঁই, গুৱাহাটী বুক ষ্টল, ১৯৭০
২। বাস্তৱৰ স্বপ্ন ড০ হীৰেণ গোহাঁই, প্ৰথম লৰ্য়াচ সংস্কৰণ, ১৯৯৬
৩। অসমীয়া মধ্যবিত্ত সমাজৰ ইতিহাস, ড০ প্ৰফুল্ল মহন্ত, পূৰ্বাচল প্ৰকাশ, গুৱাহাটী, ১৯৯১
৪। সৌৰভ কুমাৰ চলিহা আৰু অন্যান্য প্ৰবন্ধ (সম্পা), ৰঞ্জিৎ কুমাৰ দেৱগোস্বামী, সমন্বয় গ্ৰন্থালয়, নলবাৰী, ১৯৯৫
৫। অসমীয়া চুটিগল্প অধ্যয়ণ, ড০ প্ৰহ্লাদ বৰুৱা, বাণী মন্দিৰ, ১৯৯৫
৬। উপন্যাস আৰু অসমীয়া উপন্যাস, ড০ গোবিন্দ প্ৰসাদ শৰ্মা, ষ্টুডেন্টচ ষ্টোৰচ, গুৱাহাটী, ১৯৯৬
৭। এহাত ডাবা, সৌৰভ কুমাৰ চলিহা, প্ৰথম লৰ্য়াচ সংস্কৰণ, ১৯৯৫
৮। গোলাম, সৌৰভ কুমাৰ চলিহা, প্ৰথম লৰ্য়াচ সংস্কৰণ, ১৯৯৬
৯। সমীৰণ বৰুৱা আহি আছে, মনোজ কুমাৰ গোস্বামী, জাৰ্নাল এম্পৰিয়াম, নলবাৰী, ১৯৯৭
১০। ফ্ৰানজ কাফ্‌কাৰ গল্প (অনু), তৰণী ডেকা, ডেউকা চতুৰ্দ্দশ সংখ্যা, জুলাই, ১৯৯৫
১১। ডেউকা, এয়োদশ সংখ্যা, জানুয়াৰাৰী, ১৯৯৫
১২। ডেউকা, চতুৰ্দ্দশ জুলাই, ১৯৯৫
১৩। সাদিন, শাৰদীয় সংখ্যা, ১৯৮৯ৰ পৰা ১৯৯৭ লৈকে
১৪। বংঘৰ, শাৰদীয় সংখ্যা, ১৯৯৫
১৫। বুধবাৰ, শাৰদীয় সংখ্যা, ১৯৯৬

INDEX